THE GIST OF

GOLF

THE GIST OF

GOLF

HARRY VARDON

RUTLEDGE HILL PRESS®
Nashville, Tennessee

This book is a reprint of the book *The Gist of Golf* as published in the United States in 1922 by George H. Doran Company, New York, New York. The cover design, page design, and glossary were specially commissioned for this edition by Rutledge Hill Press® and are the copyrighted property of Rutledge Hill Press®.

Published in Nashville, Tennessee, by Rutledge Hill Press®, 211 Seventh Avenue North, Nashville, Tennessee 37219.

Distributed in Canada by H. B. Fenn & Company, Ltd., 34 Nixon Road, Bolton, Ontario L7E 1W2.

Distributed in Australia by The Five Mile Press Pty., Ltd., 22 Summit Road, Noble Park, Victoria 3174.

Distributed in New Zealand by Tandem Press, 2 Rugby Road, Birkenhead, Auckland 10.

Distributed in the United Kingdom by Verulam Publishing, Ltd., 152a Park Street Lane, Park Street, St. Albans, Hertfordshire AL2 2AU.

Typography by Roger A. DeLiso, Rutledge Hill Press®

Library of Congress Cataloging-in-Publication Data
Vardon, Harry, 1870–
    The gist of golf / Harry Vardon.
        p.   cm.
        Originally published: New York: Doran, c1922. With additions.
        ISBN 1-55853-750-3
        1. Golf.   I. Title.
    GV965.V33   1999
    796.352'3–dc21   98-55381
                                                      CIP

Printed in the United States of America

1 2 3 4 5 6 7 8 9–02 01 00 99

CONTENTS

ILLUSTRATIVE CHARTS

From Photographs Posed by the Author

GLOSSARY

Befitting an English gentleman, Harry Vardon, the only man to win as many as six British Open Championships, writes in a turn-of-the-century British parlance that on a few occasions can baffle English-speaking Americans. This glossary is offered as a translation guide of sorts, explaining a few terms perhaps otherwise unknown. Also included are brief biographical sketches of many of the more prominent golfers mentioned in the book. Note, too, in the main text that follows that the spelling of a number of words has been changed to reflect contemporary American spellings.

—the editor, January 1999

Auchterlonie, Willie. British Open champion in 1893.

baffy. This sturdy hickory-shafted club replaced the baffing spoon and had a lofted face for high shots from the fairway. It was similar to the modern three- or four-wood.

Balfour, Mr. Presumably, this refers to Leslie Balfour Melville, who won the 1895 British Amateur at

St. Andrews, where six years earlier he had been the runner-up in the same event.

Ball, John, Jr. (1862–1940). An outstanding amateur of his era, Ball won the British Open in 1890 and the British Amateur Championships eight times between 1888 and 1912.

Ball, Tom. British Open runner-up in 1908 and 1909.

Braid, James (1870–1950). The first golfer to win the British Open five times (between 1901 and 1910). He was one of the founders of the British PGA.

brassie. A wooden fairway club with a protective brass soleplate, the equivalent of the modern two-wood.

cleek. Term of Scottish origin describing a narrow-bladed iron driving club, roughly equivalent to the modern one- or two-iron.

cuppy lie. Golf ball lying in a small depression.

Duncan, George (1883–1964). British Open champion of 1920 who went on to play in the first three Ryder Cup Matches.

Evans, Charles "Chick" (1890–1979). One of America's great amateurs, Evans in 1916 became the first man to win the U.S. Open and U.S. Amateur Championship in the same year.

Fernie, Willie. British Open champion of 1883, despite scoring a 10 on one hole.

foozling. Managing clumsily; bungling, especially a poor stroke in golf.

gaol. Jail.

Herd, Alexander "Sandy" (1868–1944). British Open champion in 1902.

Hilton, Harold Horsfall (1869–1942). The best amateur of his era, Hilton won the British Open in 1892 and 1897, the British Amateur four times, and the U.S. Amateur once. He was also the editor of *Golf Monthly*.

howk. Dig out, figuratively speaking. To extricate from a tough lie.

jigger. A metal golf club with a narrow face.

Kirkaldy, Andrew (1860–1934). Runner-up in the British Open in 1879, 1889, and 1891, Kirkaldy was the Honorary Professional to the Royal and Ancient Club (St. Andrews) from 1910 to 1933.

Laidlay, John Ernest (1860–1940). In the 1880s and early 1890s, Laidlay was the leading Scottish amateur, winning the British Amateur Championship in 1889 and 1891 and the Scotland vs. England Championship from 1902 to 1911.

mashie. An iron club that appeared in the late 1880s, the mashie had loft equivalent to the modern five-iron.

Massy, Arnaud. Skilled golfer whose achievements included winning the 1907 British Open and participating in a British Open play-off in 1911 ultimately won by Vardon.

Maxwell, Robert. British Amateur champion in 1903 and 1909.

midiron. An iron golf club that has more loft than a driver and less than a three-iron, used for medium fairway shots and long approaches; similar to today's two-iron, but distinguished from the driving cleek (which also has been likened to a two-iron) in that it has slightly more loft.

niblick. An early lofted iron, the niblick was roughly equivalent to a modern nine-iron. With a heavy head and a wide face slanted at a greater angle than any other iron except a wedge, it was used for extricating, or "howking," the ball from difficult lies or for lofting it over hazards.

Ouimet, Francis (1893–1967). Former caddie who, as a twenty-year-old American amateur, defeated Vardon and Ted Ray in a play-off for the 1913 U.S. Open title, thus becoming the first amateur to win the event.

Park, Willie, Jr. (1864–1925). A legendary putter who won the British Open in 1887 and 1889. Park also designed golf courses and was the inventor of golf clubs and a fifty-six-sided golf ball called the Park Royal. He was the first professional to write a complete book on golf, *The Game of Golf,* in 1896.

Ray, Edward "Ted" (1877–1970). One of the longer hitters of his day, Ray won the U.S. Open in 1912 and 1920. He joined Vardon for an exhibition tour in America in 1913.

slog/slogging. Cricket term that refers to the hard-hitting antics of a batsman—the act of overswinging at the ball, trying to hit it as far as possible. Put a *u* in place of the *o* and you get slug or slugging, which is pretty much synonymous.

spoon. Traditional name for a lofted fairway wood, equivalent to a modern three-wood.

Tait, Lieutenant F. G. "Freddie" (1870–1900). Scottish amateur who won the British Amateur Championship in 1896 and 1898. A member of the Royal and Ancient Club, he was killed leading his men into battle in the Boer War at Koodoosberg Drift.

Taylor, John Henry (1871–1963). The first golfer from the legendary triumvirate of Vardon, Braid, and Taylor to come to prominence in the late nineteenth and early twentieth centuries. Taylor won the British Open five times.

Travis, Walter J. An Australian-born American, Travis took up golf at the age of thirty-five. Known as "Old Man," he won the U.S. Amateur Championship three times and the British Amateur Championship in his first and only attempt in 1904.

Wethered, R. H. "Roger." A first-class player who won the 1923 British Amateur two years after losing a British Open play-off to Jock Hutchison in 1921. Roger was the older brother of Joyce Wethered, who herself won five consecutive English Ladies Championships and four British Ladies Amateur Championships.

White, Jack. Beat out Braid and Taylor by one stroke to win the 1904 British Open.

(Sources: *The Random House International Encyclopedia of Golf*, *The American Heritage Dictionary of the English Language* (3rd edition), *Webster's Third New International Dictionary*, *Golf Magazine's Encyclopedia of Golf*, *The Historical Dictionary of Golfing Terms: From 1500 to the Present*, the PGA Tour media guide, and *The Game of Golf and the Printed Word, 1566–1985*)

THE GIST OF
GOLF

CHAPTER

I

THE DRIVING SWING

---

*With some advice concerning
clubs and the grip*

CHAPTER I

THE DRIVING SWING

*With some advice concerning
clubs and the grip*

A GREAT DEAL of unnecessarily bad golf is played in this world. The people who go on playing it, year in and year out, with unquenchable hope and enthusiasm, constitute the game's mainstay, for their zeal is complete, and zeal that remains unabated in the face of long-sustained adversity is the most powerful constituent in the whole fabric of a prosperous pastime.

All the same, these chronic sufferers from foozling would like to play better than they do. And they could play better. There is no reason why a physically sound individual, who takes up the game before old age with the determination to succeed at it, should fail to develop form justifying a tolerably low handicap—say, five or six. After that, everything must depend upon the person's inborn faculties as a golfer. As a rule, it is some very simple error of ways that retards progress, an error that becomes more or less perpetuated in the system.

There are various theories as to the best method

of learning golf. I have no hesitation in saying that the struggling player should first make himself master of the swing with the wooden clubs—the driver or the brassie. It cannot be emphasized too strongly that, for most of the shots in golf, the principles of the swing are the same. To the unpracticed eye, a first-class player may seem to wield his midiron differently from the manner in which he swings his driver, but the variation comes only of the fact that the former is the shorter club and that, therefore, he has to stand nearer to the ball for it. The effect of the shorter club and the position closer to the ball is to make the swing more upright, but the good golfer is not conscious of any effort to change his manner of swinging.

The mashie and its stout brother, the niblick, call for a swing which is rather different from the others, and the putter is a thing apart, but for all the shots from the tee and through the green until we take the mashie for pitching up to the hole, the swings are—or should be—identical in their main principles.

Before discussing the golf swing, we ought to consider the player's set of clubs and his manner of holding them. More than once I have heard amateurs say, "No wonder professionals play so well, they always pick the best clubs." It is not so much a matter of choosing the best—everybody does that—as of selecting those which are in the nature of brothers. The golfer needs what I might call a family group of clubs. The "lie"—that is, the inclination of the club as it is held on the ground in the ordinary position for striking—should be similar in his set in the sense that the full extent of the sole of each club should be capable of resting naturally on the ground when the player is standing ready for the shot.

When the heel of the club touches the ground and the toe is slightly cocked up in the air, or vice versa, the results can hardly be good. Yet thousands of golfers are influenced solely by the "feel" of a club. They will use it in spite of the fact that its "lie" is ill-adapted to their stance, and frequently when, in the end, they discard it in despair, they cannot make out what is wrong with it.

I always advise the novice, or the person who is still in the throes of foozling after several years' application to the game, to concentrate for a time on four clubs—the brassie, midiron, mashie, and putter, and to leave the mashie alone until he can use the brassie and iron with some effect.

I recommend a brassie at the start, not for playing shots from the turf, but for learning how to drive. It has a stiffer shaft than the driver, and, as a result, there is a greater chance of keeping it under control.

You want a little loft on the face of the club, so as to help in getting the ball into the air; this element of loft gives confidence to the novice, and even if sometimes there is luck in the circumstance of his making the ball rise (or if, at any rate, he would not have met with such success with a straight-faced club), the encouragement that he derives from the feat is worth a lot to him. He should accustom himself immediately to a low tee; if he succumbs to the temptation to poise the ball an inch or so clear of the ground for the drive, every shot that he has to play from the turf will seem twice as difficult to him as it should be.

It is sound policy to confine your attention to these two clubs for three weeks, assuming that you practice for an hour several times a week. If you want a change, the putter may be tried, because there is no harm in experimentation with a variety of stances and methods where this club is concerned. None of them will interfere with the fixed principles which you are trying to introduce into your system for the proper manipulation of the other instruments.

As time progresses, further clubs will be added to the bag, and a person who has been playing for two or three years ought to know what clubs suit him best. By that time he will have bought a great number in the hope of lighting on at least a few that seem divinely inspired, and very likely he will have fallen into the way of taking out with him a large collection.

There are many golfers who feel that they must have at least a dozen or fourteen. Seven or eight ought to be ample—the driver, brassie, cleek, iron, mashie, niblick, and putter, with, perhaps, a particular fancy in the way of a spoon or a jigger added to the equipment to give a sense of security. The spoon is a good substitute for the cleek when the latter proves to be in a peevish mood, and some golfers prefer the jigger to the mashie. The jigger, with its longer blade, strikes them as being the easier to use.

I confess that, on important occasions, I carry eleven clubs, but three of these are spares and are seldom employed. It is a sound argument, too, that the more moderate the player, the better chance will he have of improving by pinning his faith to a few clubs.

Now as to grip. I am told that I have acquired a reputation for laying down a kind of dogma, that nobody can hope to excel at golf unless he adopts the overlapping grip. I really do not deserve such distinction, because, while I am convinced that the grip mentioned is the best, it has never occurred to me to tell anybody that it is the only proper method. Undoubtedly, it is to be recommended very strongly to a beginner, who requires only a little patience in order to master it, but when a person has been gripping in another manner for a year or two, it is not always wise to effect a radical change in principle unless that which he favors is hopelessly incorrect. It is reasonable to consider this matter of the grip with all due regard for human fancies and foibles. But we must not lose sight of the fact that some styles of gripping are so bad as to constitute insurmountable barriers to success.

As a rule, the involuntary way in which a novice takes hold of a club is wrong because he generally holds it deeply in the palms of the two hands, with the knuckles well under the shaft, and has the hands slightly apart. These dispositions are the two archenemies of correct hitting. It is an inexorable rule that, to make the ball fly straight you must have the back of the left hand facing the way that you are going, so that it shall control the club to the extent of giving it a straight face at the impact, and that the two hands must be touching, if they are not overlapping, in order that they shall not work against one another.

These are all-important, cardinal points on which to base our mode of procedure. I take it, that in every game in which a ball has to be struck with a club, or bat, or stick, there are right and wrong ways of holding that instrument. Certainly such is the case in connection with cricket, billiards, and other pastimes which I have had opportunities of studying. But in no game is it as important as in golf, because, whereas you may conceivably score if you hit the ball in an unintended direction at cricket and the like, you cannot do the right thing by getting off the line at golf. And yet there are thousands of players who say they like to grip in the way that feels most comfortable, and that they are not going to try anything else.

It is a very unprofitable attitude to adopt. In point of fact, the way that feels most comfortable is wrong in four cases out of every five. If I were going to try to master billiards (a game of which I am very fond, but which I have few chances of playing), I would learn first to hold the cue properly. The impulse of the average player seems to be to grip it as he might seize a bludgeon with which to attack somebody; but it is noticeable that the good billiards player holds the cue lightly in his fingers. It is just this kind of difference that calls for consideration in connection with the golf grip.

Some of the absolute beginners who ask for lessons are alarming in their ideas of grip. The strangest I ever encountered was a lady who wanted to be instructed in the rudiments of the game in my garden school at Totteridge. This lady confessed that she had never played before, and she arrived with a brand new set of clubs of impressive appearance. Following my custom, I asked her to execute a few swings in the way that came naturally to her, so that I might estimate the style that suited her. I noticed that she was gripping curiously, but said nothing at the moment.

Something possessed me to stand in front of her. As a rule, I stand well to the right of a player to see the swing. She fixed her eye on the ball, and then, like a flash of lightning, pushed the club straight out in front of her. How she proposed to hit the ball in that manner I do not know; what I do know is that she very nearly hit me on the point of the jaw. If I had not jumped back, I should have caught it beautifully. That pupil had her first lesson after her first swing.

There are three golf grips which are more or less correct. One is the old-fashioned palm grip, in which the player holds the club well in the palm of the right hand, with the knuckles under the shaft, but has the back of the left hand facing the direction of play. Mr. John Ball and Alexander Herd are the most illustrious golfers I know who adopt this method, and certainly they do very well with it.

I would not dissuade any player from favoring it if he felt that it was the only way in which he could hit the ball, but it is disadvantageous in a heavy lie, because, as the club meets the turf, it is likely to turn in the right hand. There is no check on it to prevent it turning unless you hold very tightly with the right hand, and an intensely hard grip is bad for the reason that it tends to render taut all the muscles of the arm, whereas they should be flexible. However, it is possible to play some good shots with this grip, especially when the lies are clean and the ball can be picked up without the club having greater contact with the turf than to clip through the closely cropped grass. If you must adopt such a method, I would say only, "Be sure that the hands are touching."

It is a mistake to suppose that by putting the back of the right hand under the shaft, and holding the club deeply in the palm, you get more power. Or perhaps I should say that it is an error to suppose that you profit by getting more power in this manner, supposing that you do obtain it. As a matter of fact, you ought not to be conscious that the hands in particular are doing a lot of hard work. Their function is to put the clubhead into the proper position for hitting the ball, not to do the hitting. They are to all intents and purposes a connecting link between the arms and the club—nothing more. It is the swing—the swing of the club, the hands, and the arms acting as one piece of mechanism—that produces the power and makes the ball travel.

If you try to hit with the hands, you are almost sure to spoil the effort by holding too tightly with the right. The player who falls into this error generally slices. The hands in their desperation arrive opposite the ball before the clubhead reaches it, and the latter is therefore drawn across the ball. You will notice that a good golfer usually finishes with most of his weight on the right leg. That is because, having depended upon the swing to secure the distance, he drops on to the right leg to check the club. If he were to hit with his hands, his body would go forward with the follow-through, and the bulk of his weight would be on the left leg at the finish.

It is because the old-fashioned palm grip encourages—and in bad lies necessitates—a tight grip with the right hand that I think it has a defect. You need to hold a club firmly, especially with the thumbs and forefingers, but not like grim death. There is no earthly reason why so many golfers should have corns on their hands—the consequence of very tight gripping. Personally, I never have a corn on either of my hands except near the little finger of the left hand, and that is caused solely by the fact that I wear a ring on the finger mentioned. The palm gripper nearly always has a lot of corns.

So much for the ancient method of gripping, which is still very extensively practiced, especially among amateurs. The second acceptable principle represents the stage before the overlapping grip. Very little change is necessary to alter it to the latter. The club is held so that the two thumbs rest on the shaft, and, with the forefingers, form V's. The right hand, instead of being under the shaft, is brought around, and the back of that hand faces away from the line of play. The back of the left hand looks toward the line of play.

Here, then, we have the hands nicely balanced— the backs of the hands facing in opposite directions, and the thumbs and forefingers formed into V's with their apex uppermost. This is a sound grip so long as you remember to make the hands meet on the shaft. They must not be apart, even to the extent of the tiniest fraction of an inch.

To proceed from the grip described to that known as "overlapping," all that you have to do is to bring the right hand a little higher up so that the ball of the thumb rests on the back of the left thumb and the little finger of the right hand deposits itself on the forefinger of the left. In this way you make the grip more compact and render the union of the hands complete. Some people like to bring the right hand so far up that they overlap with two or three fingers of it. There is nothing to be said against the scheme if the golfer prospers on it, but personally I think that the ideal feeling of freedom is obtained when one overlaps only with that little finger of the right hand.

These, then, are the three grips suited to the game, and it is not too much to say that all others have their pronounced faults. The last feature that I like to alter in a player's methods is the way in which he disposes his hands, but sometimes it is unavoidable. When the backs of both hands are looking down to the ground (a frequent condition in the novice) it is impossible to swing the club.

There once came to me a man who gripped, with the back of the right hand looking upwards. He had to turn it in order to get the club up. In these cases it is often necessary to put a golfer completely off what he calls his game so as to enable him ultimately to play a better one. It is a point worth remembering that when the early effects of changes advised by a teacher are to make the shots seem more difficult than ever, it is often a prelude to success. When the only way to put a player right is to undo at the outset all that he has done wrong, he generally suffers a period of purgatory.

It is a rather curious circumstance that people

THE DRIVING SWING

ILLUSTRATIVE CHART

STANCE AND ADDRESS.—The grip is all important, the one I advocate being the two V overlapping grip, formed by the thumb and forefingers. To achieve this the ball of the right thumb should rest on the back of the left thumb with the little finger of the right hand over the middle joint of the forefinger of the left hand, thus bringing about a perfect union of the hands while playing. Weight evenly distributed on both legs; no stiffness of body.

BEGINNING OF UPSWING.—Head still. Note that left knee has begun to turn inward, making the body start to pivot at the hips. The left wrist also turns and with it the clubface. Throughout every stroke the eyes must be kept on the ball.

TOP OF SWING.—The left knee has continued its inward movement, while with the head kept perfectly still, the turn of the hips has been completed and the even distribution of the weight of the body maintained.

with short fingers generally choose clubs with thick handles, while players with long fingers exhibit a preference for thin handles. Where the grip is concerned, the nature of that part of the club which you are going to hold is important, and I would advise the short-fingered section of the community to select thin grips, because they generally mean better balanced clubs than thick grips. The latter are sometimes necessary in the case of a person with long fingers. Unless the handle was fairly substantial, it would be more or less lost in his hands.

Having gone into the questions of our clubs and the way we grip them, let us now diagnose the swing with the wooden club. It is the basis of successful golf.

All the good shots in the game (all, at any rate, except the putt, which is a thing apart) are founded on the principle of the body turning on a pivot instead of swaying back and then lunging forward at the ball. That pivot is the waist. No doubt everybody who has made the slightest study of golf appreciates this piece of orthodoxy, but the number of people who disregard it, even though they realize its importance, constitute about half the golfing world. Why do they fail to observe the first law of the true swing?

Presumably the reason is that in the days of their novitiate they fall into a bad habit which becomes ingrained in their constitutions. They perpetrate it without being conscious that they are practicing it. That is the way with habits. There is many a person who will declare till he is black in the face that he is not swaying, when you know all the while that he is.

It is a fallacy to suppose that any particular part of the body, such as the arms or wrists, has to be very specially applied to the task of hitting the ball. The whole anatomy should work as one piece of mechanism, with the club as part and parcel of the human frame. The clubhead should be started first by means of a gentle half-turn of the left wrist toward the body, and the arms should follow, thus causing the body to screw around at the hips until the arms will go no farther. To all intents and purposes, you wind up the body with the arms and unwind it with the same agents, your whole frame turning in such a manner that it never moves outside the space which you have allotted to it in taking up your position.

It is as though you had a neck made of indiarubber, so that it would allow the shoulders to turn without the head moving. If at this moment you stand

comfortably with your hands on your hips, toes pointing outward, and heels about fifteen inches apart, and
keeping the head absolutely still, screw the body
around at the hips and unscrew it again, you will have
a very fair idea of the proper action for the golf swing.
Only, of course, you screw it around much farther
when playing, because the freedom of the arms gives
it greater liberty to turn, and you raise the left heel—
without, however, allowing it to turn outward—so as to
ease the strain on the leg as the hips screw around.

Many golfers try to hit with the arms. That is a
mistake. The arms should be in effect simply a con-
tinuation of the shaft. During my first tour in the
United States, when the game was young in America,
there were many theories among the spectators as to
how the shots were accomplished, and I remember
particularly being cornered by a man who, just after I
had made a rather good shot, jumped the ropes and
asked excitedly of a friend beside me: "Which arm did
he do that with?" My companion put the question to
me, and I had to look for a moment to make sure that
one arm had not become shorter or longer than the
other. I do not believe there is such a thing as a master arm in the real golf swing. The two arms work as
one and as part of the entire mechanism of the body.

A common cause of swaying is a tendency to take

the club up too quickly. Once a person has become an accomplished player, the rapidity of his upswing is not necessarily a matter of great importance, because instinctively he works his body properly, but for the beginner or mediocre golfer, a fast upswing is usually fatal. It results in most cases in a hasty snatch of the clubhead from the top of the swing, and it is an invariable rule that if you start the arms first—either at the beginning or at the top of the swing—the result is bad. The clubhead must lead in each place. The wrists must give it the lead. Then the arms will follow it and do what is needed of them.

I would recommend the average golfer to practice a steady upswing, not exactly a creeping operation, but slow rather than fast. If, when experimenting without a ball, he will raise the club very slowly so as to watch just what happens and bring it down just as slowly, he will see that it comes down precisely as it goes up. It has one track. Well, now, even if he starts it properly when playing and subsequently develops such pace in the upswing that in his spirit of impetuosity he snatches the club from the top, he can be sure that it will come down on a different track from that which it followed when being raised. The arms will throw the clubhead forward and the body will begin to unwind at the hips a fraction of a second too soon, and the consequence will be disaster. Here we have the cause of more than half the foozling in the world. Once the clubhead has led from the top of the swing, its pace can be accelerated with all the vim that the player possesses. But not before.

The first thing to do is to select a comfortable stance on the teeing ground. You have a choice within prescribed limits; it is the one place where you enjoy such a privilege; and you may as well take advantage of it. All teeing grounds are not perfectly level, and it is a help to possess a feeling of even balance as you address the ball. Stand easily with a distinct sense of relaxation in the joints and muscles; if you tighten them during the upswing through a determination to make a tremendously powerful shot, you are nearly sure to ruin the swing. You have nothing to hit till you come down.

Fix your eye on the back of the ball and see that the sole of the club is completely grounded behind the object—not merely the heel of the club resting on the turf and the toe cocked up in the air. The feet can be either in line with one another, or the right foot can be a few inches in advance of the left. The latter, I think, is an advantage, because it makes the finish easier. It is fatal to have the left in front of the right, since you could never finish properly in such circumstances. The ball should not be midway between the feet; it should be decidedly nearer to the left.

If you are standing properly, the procedure which produces a satisfactory shot is simply this: The clubhead starts first, the arms follow, and the body screws around at the hips with the head kept still until the instrument is in position behind the head. Coming down, the clubhead again starts first, the arms follow, and the hips unscrew until the ball is struck, and the pace which the club has been gathering on its downward journey produces what we call the follow-through.

There are a few points of detail in connection with this operation which call for consideration. I have said earlier that you start the clubhead first by giving the left wrist a gentle half-turn toward the body. This is important, because it will put that wrist at the top of the swing into the only position in which it is capable of doing its work properly—that is, arched inward under the shaft instead of arched outward. If you turn the hips correctly, the right leg will straighten as you take the club up. You could do with a wooden leg at the top of the swing.

As something must give way to accommodate the turn of the body, the left knee bends. Consequently, the heel is raised from the ground, and as the body-turn continues the pressure on the left is sup-ported by the inside of the foot—to be precise, on that part which stretches from the big joint to the end of the big toe. Give the clubhead a start coming down before you begin to bring the arms around and then hit. The all-important matter is to get to the top prop-erly and start down properly; after that the swing will take care of itself so long as you let it go, keep your head down, and avoid wondering whether you are likely to miss the globe.

CHAPTER

II

HOW TO USE THE CLEEK

---

*With some advice on
alternative clubs*

HOW TO USE THE CLEEK

*With some advice on
alternative clubs*

THERE IS no shot in golf which gives greater joy—
I am not sure that there is any which affords such
complete satisfaction—as a well-hit ball with a cleek. It
is not an easy club to use. Many players, after trying
it more or less exhaustively and patiently, give it up in
despair and turn to an alternative club, such as the
spoon or the baffy, to solve their difficulty of reaching the green from a distance rather greater than can
be compassed with a midiron.

As a rule, they continue to carry the cleek for
appearance's sake, since it is so essentially part of the
equipment of a complete golfer, and sometimes they
are tempted to put it to the test again for one or two
shots during the round. With almost monotonous
regularity, however, does one hear them say at the
finish, "It's no good; I can't use the cleek. I must
stick to the baffy."

I am all for the golfer making the game as easy as
he can for himself by the judicious selection of clubs.

To suggest that he ought to persist with a cleek with which he hardly ever hits a good shot would be absurd. Its use may be the indication of a golfer who is determined to master the game in the approved way, but it is not compulsory.

All the same, the troubles that are experienced with it are frequently the result of disregard of small matters which can easily be set right. And it is worthwhile attempting to remedy them, and starting afresh on a course of endeavor with the cleek, because once you obtain with it a reasonable measure of confidence and certainty, there are shots at your command which give supreme joy in the playing as well as splendid results.

You can control the ball with the cleek more effectively than with the alternative clubs. When you hit it well, you know at once just where it is going to pitch. With the spoon or the baffy, there is not quite the same sense of definiteness—the same certainty of a purpose achieved—from the instant you strike the ball. Sometimes it flies a little farther than you had expected; at other times, not quite so far.

One important point with the cleek is to have a club with just a little loft on it. To be sure, you do not want much loft if it is to be really a cleek, but the virtually straight-faced clubs which one sees so often only accentuate the difficulties without producing any compensating advantage when the ball is hit perfectly.

Another matter of importance is to be sure that the head of the club is not too heavy—a cause of many failures with it. You want a fairly thick blade, but it is impossible to set down any particular weight as being the ideal, since what suits one person may be wholly unsuited to another. It is a question—a vital question—which every player must study and settle for himself, and guidance lies in the "feel" of the club when he is swinging it.

I have wielded plenty of cleeks which have provoked at once a feeling of dragging at the arms during the swing. That is a sure sign of unsuitability; yet thousands of golfers go on using such cleeks. The last one I made for myself presented a little trouble directly when I took it on to the course. In the shop it seemed perfect, but I knew there was something wrong with it from the moment I started to play. A little practice convinced me that it was too heavy, so I filed a bit off the toe. With its weight reduced, the cleek realized my expectations.

That is an indication of the small change you may make in a club and produce from it big results. It is a factor of the kind—there are many like it—to which a professional is always paying attention, because his livelihood depends in a considerable measure on his playing ability, but which amateurs are apt to ignore. If you know you are hitting the ball well—and instinctively you are usually guided to a right judgment on this question—and yet the shots are not coming off, then the chances are that there is something wrong with the club.

My experience is that no club is so liable to possess defects as the cleek. That, I believe, is why many people abandon hope of mastering it. In many instances they have never had a cleek answering to their requirements, so that they have had no real opportunity of making the best use of one of the most valuable types of clubs ever devised.

The most common defect is for the toe to possess too much weight. The result is that the club drags at you as you swing it. You may not be conscious of this circumstance, but the fact is that the toe of the club is pulling at you all the while, and having just sufficient effect on your swing to spoil the shot. It takes very little to do that; the face of the cleek has to be out of position in only an infinitely small degree at the impact for the shot to be ruined.

You cannot always trust the impression that seizes you when you obtain a cleekhead which has no shaft on it. Sometimes it seems just the thing for which you have been searching for years—until you have a shaft fitted on it, and then it suddenly loses all its charm, usually through the sudden acquirement of a measure of heaviness which had not seemed previously to exist.

The forging of cleekheads is an important and specialized industry. There are some firms who produce nothing but cleekheads. In some cases, however, I fear that the work is not so well done as it might be, and as the cleek, more, perhaps, than any other club, must be of perfect construction and adaptability to its owner, small deficiencies count for a lot—including, I dare say, the frequency of that remark, "I simply can't use a cleek."

Very much do I miss my old cleek, with its stumpy, thick-set head. It was a Carruthers club, and a thing of joy to me. I used it for years; somehow its weight seemed to be ideally distributed—and concentrated—in that stumpy head. I could "push" the ball very far and very low with it, and know from the moment I hit the ball exactly where it was going to pitch. You never have quite that pleasure with a lofting shot. You may play it well, but it lacks the exhilaration of the low-lying stroke with the cleek, in which you strike the ball boldly and strongly, and seem somehow to have it on a bit of string all the while, so that, as it nears its objective, its velocity fades away and it drops lifeless beside the hole.

That is golf in all its glory. It is the strong wine of the game, and I say in all sincerity, that the person who has not experienced it knows not the pinnacle of pleasure to which this wonderful pastime can raise its devotee.

It is better, perhaps, to pay your homage to the cleek before you reach the sere and yellow of life. It calls for a fine confidence, a suppleness of the muscles, and a trueness of hitting that are not given to all of us in our later years. But it is never too late to try and master it. There are times when the system seems perfectly attuned to it. It came back to me in a very gratifying degree in 1920 when, at fifty, I was playing my cleek shots pretty well—if not, indeed quite as well—as in 1898 and 1899, when I really could hit a ball with any club.

I would ask the reader who wishes to make a good friend of a good cleek, first to digest the principles of grip and swing that I have put forward in the advice on driving. Once you have taken up your position, you need not be conscious of trying to do anything very different with the cleek from the procedure which you follow when playing a full shot with a wooden club. The grip; keeping the head still; the

THE CLEEK
ILLUSTRATIVE CHART

STANCE AND ADDRESS.—As the parallel lines on the mat indicate, the player is a little nearer to the ball than for the drive. Feet also slightly closer together, otherwise position similar to that for the driver.

BEGINNING OF UPSWING.—Similar movement as that for the start of the upswing with the driver. The chief point of difference is the fact that, being nearer to the ball, the swing is necessarily more upright.

TOP OF SWING.—With the exception that the club does not go quite so far back as for the driver, the position of the body at this stage should be identical with that for the driver.

importance of giving the clubhead its start with a half-turn of the left wrist, so that it leads the operation, with the arms following, and the body then screwing around at the hips so as to avoid a sway—all these points apply as much to the ordinary cleek shot as to the driver shot. Only, as the clubs are of different length and construction, a slight difference in the stance is necessary

In the ordinary way, the cleek is two or three inches shorter than the driver or brassie. Consequently, you must stand a little nearer to the ball, so as to play the shot comfortably. I am not sure that it is wise to set down distances in inches and fractions of inches. I have experimented a good deal with my own stance. With sand on the ground to mark the position of my feet, I have played half a dozen shots of exactly the same kind at intervals so short as only to give me time to step a yard away from the position and return to it. No two stances have been precisely the same, although the variations have been so slight as to be negligible.

What the golfer must do is to develop an instinct for the right stance—an instinct born of practice and experience. If I give some measurements now, I would ask you to take them as examples of a general principle—not necessarily to be observed to the last quarter of an inch. Much must depend upon the build of the player.

For a full drive, I stand fairly open, with the right foot about six inches in advance of the left. For an ordinary cleek shot—not the low-flying, backspin shot, which is a difficult one, and can be described later—my right foot is only about two and a half inches in advance of the left. And, in addition to standing squarer, I am considerably nearer to the ball.

Let us suppose we have the ball in position, with a line extending on either side of it, indicating the line which the shot is to take. For a drive, the toes of my left foot—turned appreciably outward—are 33 inches from that line. The right foot—at right angles to the line—is 26 inches from it. For an ordinary cleek shot, my left foot—turned outward in about the same degree—is 24 inches from the line, and the right is 21 1/2 inches from it. In short, I have closed in on the ball to the extent of about 9 inches with the left foot and 5 inches with the right. I am that much nearer to it. It is a lot, and in an approximate measure, the difference must be observed if the shot is to be a good one.

One sees people standing in all sorts of ways for strokes with the cleek. It is small wonder that many of them fail. Some are straddle-legged and so far from the ball that they can only sweep the club around at it like a man mowing grass with a scythe. Some stand far too near, with the result that they are too cramped to play the shot effectively. A golden rule to remember is that the golfer should stand just near enough to ground the entire sole of the club from toe to heel comfortably on the turf during the address, without having to strain forward to do it or tuck his arms into his body in the process. But—the cleek being two or three inches shorter than the driver—you must be considerably nearer to the ball than for the full bang with the wooden clubs. Only in that way can you control the club perfectly, and produce that upright, concise swing which is an essential of success with the cleek.

The feet are drawn a little closer together in their relation to one another, as well as nearer to the ball. The arms should not be allowed to touch the body, but if you stretch them forward, you are sure to lose your balance. They must have just nice room to swing through comfortably as the club descends. The result of all this must be a shorter and more upright swing than is produced with the driver. It is more concise, more incisive a stroke.

In ordinary circumstances, I would say: Never practice a full swing with the cleek. The most effective shot of all—because it lends itself best to complete control—is that made with a half-swing. A three-quarter swing may be tried when there is need to get a little bit extra out of the shot, but a full swing is wholly inconsistent with the build of the club and the way in which we stand in the use of it.

It is as well to grip just a little more tightly with the cleek than with the driver. When you are hitting a ball from the tee, there is little likelihood of the club coming into contact with the ground. At least, it is an atrociously bad shot from a tee that finds the club digging into the turf. In playing a cleek shot through the green, however, the ball has to be lifted from the turf, and although the proper way is to take it cleanly, only just grazing the soil, misjudgment to the extent of an infinitesimal fraction of an inch may cause the clubhead to catch in the ground and turn in the hands. Consequently, while I am all in favor of a light grip for golf—a finger grip which keeps the club steady without allowing the palms to hold it like grim death—I am ready to admit that a slightly firmer grip may be adopted for the cleek. But I am far from agreeing with those who say that the hold should be a really tight one.

This policy of the clasping, clutching hand is not good for any shot in the game save, perhaps, when the

ball is buried in a sand bunker and you are merely trying to howk it out a few yards by creating a wholesale
disturbance in the sand behind the ball. In the ordinary way, the tight grip creates a tautening of all the
muscles in the body, and when the player is in that
condition, the chances of executing a perfect stroke
are remote. The golfer's muscles should be at once
healthy and supple—like a boxer's. When they are
encouraged to develop hardness and size—like a
weight lifter's—they retard the ease and quickness of
hitting which count for so much at the instant of the
impact. It is quite sufficient to grip a little tighter with
the thumbs and forefingers. They will prove sufficient
to keep the clubhead in position. The other fingers
may be left to look after themselves in the matter of
the strength that they apply. They are quite powerful
enough—remember, for instance, how strongly you
can clutch anything with the little finger alone—without being goaded to do their utmost in the grip.

I have found it a good plan with the cleek to aim
at a spot half an inch or even an inch behind the ball.
You know the little gap that you see when you ground
the club in the address preparatory to playing the
shot. Very likely you put the cleek down half an inch
behind the ball. Well, that is the place on which to
focus your vision—not the ball itself. Then you are

more likely to strike it cleanly instead of topping it—
that very common fault with the cleek.

It is a club with which you must hit unfalteringly.
That, indeed, is true of any implement in the golfer's
kit, for to try and regulate the strength of the shot at
the instant of impact is nearly sure to be fatal. No
matter what the club you are using, once you have
reached the stage when you feel that the upswing
should stop and have started to come down, then you
have laid the foundation of the shot for better or for
worse, and you must go through with it; the pace of
the clubhead increasing as it nears the ball so that
you are ever conscious that it is leading—that it is having its own way—and that you are merely guiding it,
content to let it hit the ball with all the vim that it has
gathered during the downswing.

I mention the point particularly in connection with
the cleek, because it is, I think, the club which more
than any other tempts a lot of players to try and regulate the strength of the shot at the impact. That may be
because they have not enough faith in themselves.
They have just a little fear of a club with an almost
straight face, and feel that they ought to make sure of
striking the ball accurately. To think of that just before
the impact is to take pains too late in the operation.

Picture the good cleek players whom you have

seen—Mr. John Ball, Mr. Harold Hilton, and the late Mr. John Garham, for instance, among the amateurs, and nearly every professional who has won an Open Championship—and remember the "nip" with which each of them has played his cleek shots. There has been no hesitancy; the club has come down at the ball with the momentum of a flywheel working its unimpeded easiest.

You may—and probably will—be thinking hard as you take the club up, and even as you start to bring it down. You may be thinking hard at that moment at the top of the swing when the club is recovered from behind your head—a movement of infinitesimal duration, but great importance, since it directs the clubhead for a brief fraction of a second straight back (in a line parallel with the line of play, only away from it) instead of forward. It is on the completion of this little but vital movement that the real hit begins, and it is at this point that you must trust to the clubhead and let it go through with all its force.

The strength of the shot must be governed by the length of the backswing. Some players—perhaps it would be fair to say the majority—use the cleek exactly as they do the driver. If they have a full swing with the driver, then they have a full swing with the cleek. That is wrong. It does not suit the latter club. A certain element of floundering nearly always asserts itself at the top of the swing—the diligent onlooker observes a semblance of a wobbling of the clubhead there, indicative of its being out of control.

The limit for the cleek should be a three-quarter swing—compact, well-knit, and without any trace of indecisiveness in it. Even that length of swing should only be attempted when you are a good player, with faith in your ability to control the club. The ideal is a half-swing—perhaps a generous half-swing. There is no reason why any golfer should fail to acquire a tolerable degree of mastery over the half-shot with a cleek, and it is a very valuable shot indeed to have in your bag. It covers a lot of ground without involving undue effort; it renders possible a measure of accurate placing of the ball which is not presented in quite the same degree by any other club in the outfit; it is a soul-satisfying shot which begets confidence; and it paves the way to the playing of the best and most gratifying shot in the game—that which is generally known as the "push," and which causes the ball to rise sharply, fly in one plane and, when its strength expires, drop lifeless beside its target, brought to its sudden standstill by the influence of the backspin that could not assert itself earlier because of the supremacy of the initial velocity.

From time to time I have recommended the moderate golfer to pin his faith to a few clubs, and I do not propose now to suggest a departure from that principle. If he focuses his attention at the start on the brassie (for tee shots), midiron, mashie, and putter, and then adds the driver, cleek, and niblick, he will make much more rapid progress than if he experiments in his foozling days with a variety of instruments of all shapes and lofts.

When the writer of these hints could play golf considerably better than he can today, and championship winning was much less of a struggle than it has been in recent years, he used nothing but the driver, brassie, cleek, midiron, mashie, niblick, and putter. Seven clubs were ample. But to live the golfing life without ever taking a fancy to something new and strange is hardly human and when a player comes to be tolerably content with his doings with what we may call the standard set, he is justified in trying some of the alternative clubs that are produced for the benefit of individuals who believe in the efficacy of a change.

So far as concerns the average golfer, I agree that the most difficult club to use is the cleek. The face of the club is shallow and almost straight, and unless the ball is struck absolutely accurately, the result is sure to be unsatisfactory. Consequently, if you feel that you will never be able to master it unless you have a rest from it, by all means resort to a substitute. The best substitute is a spoon or a driving mashie, and of the two, I recommend the former. The spoon (or the "baffy," as a slight variation of it is called) is, for the mediocre player, just about the easiest club to wield in the whole range of instruments. Moreover, it has a venerable antiquity. It was employed very extensively by old-time golfers at St. Andrews and elsewhere. In a set of ancient clubs you will generally come across a spoon. By no means, then, is it a modern subterfuge, and although for some years it has been regarded as something of a curiosity in a bag, the cleek having come to be considered orthodox, I see no reason why it should not be used extensively.

For several seasons I never went out without such a club, and never employed any with better effect. There are people who, whenever they write to me even now, ask when I am going to bring out the spoon again. Certainly it was not discarded because it ever failed me; it has merely been put among the reserves because I feel that the cleek, well used, is the proper club.

A spoon has the loft of a midiron, which gives the

player confidence in his ability to make the ball rise, and its broad sole is a help in the sense that it glides over the turf instead of digging in, as a cleek does, when the swing is not made quite properly. In short, many a shot that would be, for this reason, a complete foozle with the cleek, meets with a fair measure of success when the spoon is in use. That you get the requisite distance in spite of the fact that the loft is that of a midiron, is the natural outcome of the head of wood with the usual lead-weighting at the back.

The spoon makes the ball rise so well that it usually drops with very little run; and you can "cut" a ball to make it fall dead more easily with this club than any other, with the possible exception of the mashie. Indeed, owing to the loft, you are apt to introduce a suspicion of "cut" without trying for it. For a full shot, the swing is the same as with a driver, and it is the only wooden club with which half- and three-quarter shots can be attempted with safety by a moderate golfer. Of late there have been some signs of a revival of the popularity of the spoon, and the circumstance is not surprising. A crack player may not stand in much need of the club, but to the man who finds the successful handling of the cleek an exasperating problem, it is often a deliverer from stress.

If you prefer a driving mashie (or a driving iron

as some people term it, there is really no difference
between the two) as an alternative to the cleek, be
sure that you select one with a little loft on the face.
Sometimes the driving mashie is made with virtually
no loft at all. You do not want a lot, because, in that
case, you will not obtain the necessary distance, but
if you have none, the club is adapted for the use only
of a champion. There are plenty of driving mashies
with faces straighter than that of the average cleek,
and they are a source of trouble rather than assis-
tance to the medium and long (high) handicap players to whom they belong. Their attraction is that they
have a deep face which, compared with the narrow
face of the cleek, makes them look simple to use, but
they would be appreciably easier if they had a reasonable degree of loft. A club of this sort may be a
help to the ordinary golfer. If he decides to place his
trust in it, he should turn the cleek temporarily out
of the bag. He does not want the two; between them
he would become confused. A first-class player does,
however, usually carry two cleeks, one practically
straight-faced and the other slightly lofted. All these
are clubs for long shots, and the longest of all is to be
obtained with the straight-faced driving mashie—
when you hit the ball perfectly. But it is not used
much nowadays.

There are some veritable treasures among what are known as "mongrel" clubs—instruments with heads that have been hammered or evolved in some other way so that they present a loft and depth and weight that places them in no particular category in the standard set. Often they appeal to some trait in one's temperament or swing as nothing else could do, and I am not ashamed to admit that the pet of my bag was for many years a mongrel.

It was a cross between a cleek and a midiron, and sufficiently different from either as to present itself in the nature of a solution to a problem when one could not be quite confident as to which of those two clubs to take. I have had it for more years than I like to remember, and the head long ago became so light from constant cleaning with sandpaper that something had to be done to adjust the weight. Consequently, I had a square piece of steel fixed at the back. Reluctantly, I have had to place it on the retired list because of its old age, but I often look at it, and wish that I could press it into service again. Often when I was using it, people said to me, "What's that funny bit stuck on the back of your club?" referring to the piece of metal which I had affixed to it. But there was nothing else to be done if this mongrel was to remain in service.

And, upon my word, I would not part with it for any amount of money. I have had it since my early championships, a quarter of a century ago. The sole is round, and the head, while being slightly shorter than that of a cleek, is longer than that of a midiron. It came from America at a time, perhaps, when manufacturers in the United States had no particular idea as to the shapes, and weights, and sizes, that legitimate golf clubs should assume. I bought it in London soon after its import, being impressed mainly by its oddity and have tried many times to get it copied.

Every attempt has been a failure, although I have now another good "mongrel." One moral of this little experience is that, if you have an iron club of which the face seems perfect but the weight too light, you can safely have a piece of metal added to the head. It is a very simple matter.

Without doubt, the finest shot in the game—the stroke which gives the player the maximum of satisfaction when he has learned how to accomplish it, and without a knowledge of which nobody realizes to the full the joy that is in golf—is that which is colloquially called the "push" shot. Why it possesses this title is a matter over which we need not stop to inquire. As the push shot we know it, although there is not really any push about it, since it is simply an iron shot to which the greatest possible degree of backspin has been imparted.

The ideal club with which to play it is the cleek, although, to be sure, it is practicable with the mid-iron, the mashie, and the niblick, and not out of the question with wooden clubs. There is a touch of the push shot about nearly everything that a first-class player does with any iron club, because its object is to invest the ball with so much "stop" that its place of alightment shall be to all intents and purposes the place at which it pitches. There is no pleasure in the game like that of feeling the instant you have struck the ball that you have played this shot perfectly, so that the ball will rise quickly, fly in virtually one plane for the whole duration of its passage through the air, and then—when its initial velocity is spent and the backspin becomes the stronger influence—fall as sharply as it had risen, and finish with only a few yards of run.

Naturally, it requires practice. I do not recommend it to the man who says he plays golf only for fun—there is really nobody quite so frolicsome as that, although plenty of people pretend to be when they have been beaten by 6 & 5. Still, it is a shot for the earnest student of methods who wants to be a good player, and the club with which to practice it is the cleek.

Of first importance is the stance. The player must stand nearer to the ball than for the ordinary cleek shot—he must close in on the ball to the extent of several inches—because his object is not to hit behind the ball and propel it high into the air, but to come down on the back of it by means of an upright swing which in itself necessitates this close stance to the ball.

The stance must be more forward, too, than for the ordinary shot. When you are in the position of address, with the club grounded just behind the ball, the hands must be an inch or two in front of the ball. Moreover, the vision must be directed, not on the turf just behind the ball, but on the back of the ball itself.

You see then the manner of striking the object for which you are shaping. You are nearer to the ball than before, with the hands actually in front of it as you prepare for the shot, and you are going to perform something in the nature of a straight up-and-down swing—as nearly that as the arms will allow in comfort. You are not going to permit any waste or exuberance in the swing; you are going to take it to the top of a half- or three-quarter swing by the shortest track you know that is consistent with rhythm and ease of movement, and come down on the back of the ball. You are going to "try and bang the back out of the ball," if one may so describe it. Even though you are hitting it forward, you must be conscious that you are beating it down rather than lifting it up, as is the case in the ordinary shot.

Opinions differ as to the exact part of the ball which is struck at the impact. Some think it is just below the center; others that it is the center itself. Whichever it may be, I know my feeling is that the top half of the face of my cleek—which has been tilted slightly forward in the address, as already described—strikes the ball above the center, and that the bottom half of the clubface gets under the ball and raises it.

Anyway, the cause does not matter a lot. The effect is the main thing.

As I have said, you want to feel that you are beating the ball down as the clubhead goes through with the shot, and, as you strike, you should stiffen your wrists and let your body go forward a few inches with the club. That will help in the beating-down process, and the turf will—or should—be grazed just in front of the spot where the ball was resting.

It may be that at first the seeker of success with the push shot will suffer the tribulations of topping. But sooner or later he will hit a good one, and then he will know the feel of it—never to forget it.

HOW TO USE THE MIDIRON

*With some hints on different
shots for different lies*

CHAPTER III

HOW TO USE THE MIDIRON

*With some hints on different
shots for different lies*

THE MIDIRON is, without doubt, the handiest club in the golfer's kit, and, on the whole, the easiest to use. If I had to choose one club—and one only—with which to play a complete round, I would select unhesitatingly my midiron.

It is constantly coming in useful, and it is even more valuable to the moderate golfer than to the champion, although I can hardly imagine what any of us would do without it. Just remember how often you find yourself between 120 to 170 yards from the hole, which is roughly the midiron range. It happens repeatedly; at many holes after a good drive, and at many others after a foozle which has left you farther from the green than you should be as the result of two shots. A lot of people take a mashie and, with a full swing, hit for all they are worth. If only they would repose their faith in the midiron and play a nice, easy, well-controlled shot with it, they would fare very much better.

69

It is a club that frequently comes splendidly to the rescue when the lie of the ball is unfavorable when you are in long grass not quite lank and formidable enough to justify the use of a niblick, and when you find your ball sitting up—as you do sometimes—in a bunker and not too near the face of the hazard. It is a club with a face lofted in just that degree which makes you feel sure of getting the ball up with it, and the confidence thus begotten is priceless. Moreover, you know that you can obtain a considerable distance with it.

I suppose it is used more often than any other club for the tee shots to short holes—the ever-increasing numbers of short holes, of which there are four or five on a good many modern greens. In wintertime, when the clay courses are soft and sticky, it is invaluable for the shots through the green. A mistake that thousands of golfers make under such conditions is that they try to hit a full shot with a brassie or a nearly straight-faced iron club, such as a cleek or a driving mashie, even though they know they must follow it up with a mashie pitch, however well they may accomplish the full bang.

In point of fact, they seldom do accomplish it well; the ball lies too closely to the soft turf for such a shot to be practicable in many instances. They would find themselves much better off in the end if they were to substitute two midiron shots for their ideal of a brassie shot and a mashie chip. I know from experience that the ideal has a way of ending in sorrow on heavy clay courses, where the brassie simply will not pick the ball up cleanly from the muddy ground.

As a rule the midiron is about two inches shorter in the shaft than the cleek. It is so essentially a standard type of club—with just that degree of loft that makes a club look inviting as well as businesslike, and a depth of face that also helps in the good work of promoting confidence—that one midiron is in appearance very like another. It is for every player to find for himself the midiron that suits him; he can usually obtain a good deal of help in this matter by consulting the professional of his club, who knows his stance and any other little individualities that his golf may possess. Once he has secured the midiron that he likes, every five minutes that he spends practicing with it will be time well spent.

As the shaft of the club is shorter than that of the cleek, naturally it is necessary to stand nearer to the ball than for a cleek shot. This is an obvious—though often neglected—point. The various lengths of shafts in the golf equipment are regulated by a well-thought-out regard for the degree of uprightness with which each club in the set can be swung to the best advantage, and the golfer should remember that for every inch that is lacking in the length of the shaft he must be a little nearer to the ball during the address, so as not to strain forward to reach it.

In my own case, the right foot is about eight inches nearer to the ball than for a cleek shot and the left foot about three inches nearer. Thus my stance is more open—that is, the body is turned more toward the hole—and the feet are also closer together. This opening of the stance as you draw nearer to the ball facilitates the accomplishment of the swing for iron clubs. The swing becomes—or should become—more upright the shorter the distance that you have to make the ball travel, and the greater the need that exists for the perfect control of the length of the shot.

Having adapted your stance to the change of club, you should swing with the iron just as you do with the cleek and, indeed, even the driver, although naturally you will not swing so far back as with the latter—a longer club with which you stand so very much farther from the ball.

The midiron does its best work, I think, when it is played with a half-swing. The distance that it will make the ball travel depends upon the length of the upswing and the consequent pace at which the club-head is traveling as it comes down and strikes the ball; but in practice it is best to adopt the half-swing. If you want to extend it to a three-quarter swing in playing a later shot, do so, but I am a very profound disbeliever in straining to get the last possible yard out of a club of restricted range. I would rather take a club that is meant to make the ball travel farther—for instance, a cleek or a spoon—and play a comfortable shot with that than try to force the midiron to attain the very limit of its capacity.

It is generally agreed that professionals are better players than amateurs. Especially is this the case in Britain. Not since 1897 has an amateur won the British Open Championship, although Mr. R. H. Wethered was very near to it this year. It is the truth, however, that as a body first-class amateurs do not play so well as first-class professionals.

What is the reason? Simply, I think, that they do not play their iron shots so well as their predecessors, mainly because they have made a fetish of full swinging with iron clubs—that is, selecting the implement with which they can just secure the distance if they hit with all their might. That way lies loss of control. It stands for the biggest error in the whole gamut of golf tactics—making hard work of the game instead of taking it easily and securing better results for the absence of neck-or-nothing endeavor.

When I had my baptism of championship thrills at Prestwick in 1893, there were three amateurs in the first nine, Mr. J. E. Laidlay gaining second place, two strokes behind the winner, Willie Auchterlonie. That was a fairly common kind of occurrence. It has happened at least once since that no amateur has so much as survived the qualifying rounds of the championship.

Certainly the main difference does not lie in putting. I should say that amateurs are better putters than professionals—and ought to be. Putting is a matter not only of skill. It is a trial of nerves. The "jumps" that I have had in my right arm when I have been faced by four-foot putts, on the holing or missing of which, has depended (on) at least some measure of my reputation as an efficient professional!

There was profound truth in the remark that Alexander Herd made to an amateur who had nearly beaten him by getting down six long putts in a round. "Mon!" he said at the finish, "ye wouldna' putt like that if ye had to do it for a living."

Nor is it in driving that the professional asserts definite superiority, although I think that, on the whole, he is a little the straighter and steadier from the tee—that he hits the smaller number of crooked drives. It is in the iron shots of all lengths up to the hole that the main difference is to be found.

The professional has discovered—and in Britain he began to discover it a good many years ago—that the most successful way to play golf is the easiest way. When he has an iron shot to accomplish, he selects for the purpose the club that will enable him to achieve it with the minimum of effort. He does not take one with which he will have to execute a full swing and force for all he is worth just to reach the green—even assuming that he hits the ball truly in such desperate circumstances. Instead, he chooses a club of longer range, plays a half- or three-quarter shot over which he has complete control all the while, and puts his ball comfortably onto the green.

The number of amateurs one sees making the game as hard as they can possibly make it for themselves, by choosing an iron club which will call for an enormous effort if they are to obtain the necessary carry, is astounding. I think that, in a very large measure, this tendency is born of a pardonable but not profitable form of vainglory. There are a great many amateurs who like to say of this, that, or the other hole (to which the professional plays a drive and an iron), "I got up there today with a drive and a mashie."

Well, it may be exhilarating golf—when it comes off—and the amateur is entitled to pursue the methods that give him the greatest joy. But it is not the kind of golf that succeeds in the end. The reason that amateurs are inferior to professionals as iron-shot players is that the former so often underclub themselves in their happy-hearted desire of being able to announce triumphantly that they have accomplished a shot of 160 yards with a mashie or a jigger. It sounds exciting, but it means that they have been overswinging, and that is bound to lead to the golfing grave more often than to golfing glory.

Sometimes it is said that the estimates of a few years ago as to the distances that should be attempted with a mashie are woefully below the mark—that nowadays it is easy to get 150 yards with such a club. And you would think so, watching the number of people who attempt it. At least, you would think so until you counted the cost in unsuccessful shots. I always contend that, in normal circumstances, a golfer is ill-advised in taking his mashie at a greater distance than about 110 yards; that beyond such a range he fares better when he plays an easy shot with a midiron. And the professional golfer knows it. That is why he excels with the iron clubs, for the principle is the same in all the questions of choice of clubs for iron shots.

Occasionally, these efforts to do mighty things with iron clubs adapted for sober treatment meet with success for a whole round. But the magic does not extend to a second round. In a recent open amateur tournament in Britain, a man of fairly long handicap won the qualifying competition easily, with a very low net score, by using his favorite jigger at every conceivable distance within 160 yards of the green. He adopted the same policy in the first round of the match stages and lost nearly every hole.

I noticed that in the Oxford and Cambridge match of 1920 at Sunningdale, Mr. C. J. H. Tolley used his mashie-niblick for the second shots to the seventeenth and eighteenth holes. Far though he may have driven at these excellent two-shot holes, and admirably as the mashie-niblick may have served him on this occasion, I am certain that his tactics would fail in the aggregate if he adopted them every time in a dozen rounds. If I had been in his place, I would have taken a midiron and played the shot in comfort.

Even if two out of every three mighty swipes with iron clubs come off, they would not represent the best golf, because you would have done just as well with less forceful shots played with clubs of longer range—and probably the third shot would have come off, too.

If you keep within yourself with the iron clubs,

you have a chance of learning the way to apply back-spin. You have no chance of doing this when you are hitting with all your might. Often it is said that professionals are better iron players than amateurs, because the former can invest the ball with backspin and make it stop within reasonable distance of where it pitches. That is only possible for the reason that the professionals do not overswing; that they have control over the club throughout the movement.

When you are forcing an iron shot, you need an absolutely perfect lie. Sometimes, even on the most beautifully cut fairway, you detect just behind the ball a trifling extra growth of grass—just a long, fat bunch of grass, perhaps imperceptible to the crowd. If you are likely to come into contact with this growth in swinging through to the ball, do not attempt to force the shot. Often it is sufficient to spoil the effort.

Among amateurs, the best iron players I have seen are Mr. Charles Evans in America, and Mr. Hilton, Mr. John Ball, Mr. Robert Maxwell, and Mr. R. H. Wethered in Britain. They avoid the fatal error of underclubbing themselves; particularly is this noticeable at short holes, where the test of the iron shots stands out in bold relief. Why it is that many an amateur who cannot be sure of driving 200 yards with a wooden club, will insist upon taking a cleek and forcing for all he is worth at a hole of 195 yards—simply because it is a hole of that length—is one of the little mysteries of golf. And yet it is exactly his policy with all the iron clubs.

Where you know it will need a full swing with a mashie to achieve a certain distance, leave the mashie alone, and take your midiron.

If already you have paid me the compliment of reading my chapters on how to use the driver and the cleek, you know all I can say as to how to grip and swing the midiron—for the last-mentioned club calls for no innovation, save that you get a little nearer to the ball in the address.

Personally, I stand "open" in about this degree: Drawing a line through the ball along the intended line of flight, my left foot—pointing outward—is twenty inches from that line. My right foot—square to the line—is thirteen inches from it. Thus the right foot is seven inches in front of the left, which means that the body is turned appreciably toward the hole. Owing to the left foot pointing outward, the ball is only about three inches inside the left heel. This is the stance for any ordinary midiron shot.

In this chapter it is appropriate to deal with the different kinds of "lies" that a golfer may encounter in the course of his round. When he is lying unfavorably and wants to obtain as much length as possible, the chances are that he will take his midiron. With its generous loft and the confidence that it inspires, the club is admirably adapted to the purpose of lifting the ball from little indentations in the turf and other perplexing places.

Directly we have hit a shot and set forward in the direction of the ball, we start to wonder in what manner of lie we shall find it. Will it be cupped, or sitting up, or hanging, or on an incline? There is no other game in which these questions arise, and it is because golf has so much of the primitive about it, in spite of all the science that is applied to it, that it has a fascination which is peculiar among pastimes. We know when we have struck a shot well, and we feel that the ball ought to be lying favorably, but there is always the chance that we shall have to take some untoward condition into account. Similarly, from an indifferent shot, we may find the situation of the ball unexpectedly pleasant.

In the course of a round, the luck in this respect is generally fairly equally divided, and I have never heard of a good golfer losing a match or a medal com-

THE MIDIRON

ILLUSTRATIVE CHART

STANCE AND ADDRESS.—Still a little nearer to the ball, and feet a trifle closer than for the cleek. Observe, by comparing the chalk lines on the mat in the driver and cleek lessons, the extent to which the feet have moved forward.

BEGINNING OF UPSWING.—The left knee has bent slightly less than for the cleek. The reason for this is the fact that the midiron, being the shorter club, entails a more upright swing.

TOP OF SWING.—Notice that it is no more than a three-quarter swing. The turn of the body has been the same as for the previous shots, but the club has not gone back so far, on account of the fact that the midiron naturally accommodates itself best to this length of swing.

petition through sheer misfortune in the matter of his lies. But I dare say that many a person, playing most of his shots quite well enough to win, has been beaten because of lack of knowledge as to how to act in certain situations. Be it remembered that when the ball is lying otherwise than well poised on a level piece of turf, there is need for consideration as to what special steps shall be taken to deal with it.

That is just what the average player does not appreciate. Only when his ball is in a bunker, or a ditch, does he realize that his stance and manner of hitting must differ from the ordinary if he is to get well away. There are little traps for the unwary at many parts of the course. They are found in the variety of lies that every golfer encounters on a course that is not so flat and featureless as to be dull.

There is much difference of opinion as to the best way to stand for uphill and hanging lies. Many people do not bother at all about the matter (they just take up their ordinary stance), but it is certain that when a ball is on a slope, the stroke needs to be tackled in a manner rather different from the customary. I know good golfers who say that when the ball is hanging—that is to say, resting on a downhill slope—you should stand rather more behind the ball than usual, with most of the weight on the right leg, and the body turned well toward the hole, so as to secure the effect of a cut shot. Their argument is, that if you stand with the ball midway between your feet, the slope will carry your weight forward as you bring the club down, with the result that you will smother the ball.

This may be all very well for a short shot with a mashie, but when it is necessary to hit a long shot with an iron, I believe in standing a trifle more forward than usual. In fact, it is a safe rule in all circumstances. When your body is behind the ball, where the ground is higher, there is a very considerable chance of the club coming into contact with this part of the slope before it reaches the ball, and that can only spell ruination to the shot. When you stand a trifle in front, there is far less likelihood of hitting the turf behind the ball, although I agree that it is good to be conscious of having a little more weight than usual on the right leg in order to avoid losing the balance at the time of impact.

For an uphill lie, my own method is to stand a little more behind the ball than in the ordinary way, so as to avoid digging into the turf in front as the ball is hit. It is easy to come into contact with this rising ground. You are at the bottom of the arc of the swing at the impact, and if you stand forward, as some people do for an uphill lie, the position of the body will tend to keep the clubhead low for a fraction of a second—long enough, at any rate, to catch the ground.

It is very interesting to play on a course where one hardly ever has the same kind of stance for two shots in succession. A golfer who thinks can always adjust his stance to the situation; the chief points to remember are, as I have already stated, to stand behind the ball for an uphill lie and forward for a hanging lie. Of British championship courses, Deal gives a far bigger variety of stances than any other, but it is recognized as one of the fairest tests of golf in the land.

Its undulations are not quite so numerous as those of the Briad Hills course at Edinburgh, which gave Andrew Kirkaldy, the St. Andrews professional, very curiously to think on the occasion of his first visit to it. Halfway around somebody asked him how he was playing. "Playing?" he echoed. "How d'ye think I should be playing? I'm no' a goat!" Report says that in the afternoon Kirkaldy took out with him a large slab of turf in order to level up some of the stances.

I do not believe that; but I do remember a very cute dodge to which he resorted when eight of us took part in a tournament on Lord Dudley's private course at Witley Court, in Worcester. It was midwinter, and snow lay several inches deep upon the ground. Every ball became as slippery as slippery could be. Kirkaldy was then instructor to Lord Dudley, and wanted to do especially well in this competition—as he did—so he hit upon the idea of anointing his caddie's hair with oil and rubbing the ball into his faithful henchman's locks before playing every hole. That scheme undoubtedly saved him a lot of strokes.

A cuppy lie calls for at least a few moments' consideration, since there are two ways in which the shot may be tackled. When the ball is only slightly cupped, it is just as easy to cut through the turf behind it in order to get at the object as to make a direct stroke at it. This shot, be it said, can be played with a brassie, although many golfers imagine that when the ball is in even the slightest indentation, it is useless to think of using a wooden club. All that is necessary is to aim an inch or two behind the ball, the distance in the rear being governed by the player's instinctive estimate as to the measure of the cup's edge which he needs to cut away in order to get at the ball.

Of course it is hopeless to try and slice off a large chunk of turf, nor would I suggest to the golfer that he should do such a thing, even if it were profitable to him. Sufficient divots are raised in the ordinary way without anybody advising the extraction of more; and as moderate players are far more destructive in this respect than good golfers, I want to emphasize that nothing in the nature of an uplifting of substantial lumps of earth is advised.

It is a pity that the world of caddying is not full of zealots with tongues so caustic as that of a man whom I once heard addressing his employer on a London course.

"Did I hear you say you came from Australia?" he asked of the player, who had howked up about a dozen huge divots in a few holes.

"Yes," was the reply, "I'm from down under."

"Well," said the caddie, "if you go on like this, you'll soon be home."

It would be sacrilegious to encourage this kind of despoilment, but it is as well that golfers should know the possibilities of cutting through the top of the turf (just slicing the grass off where it protrudes from the ground) when the ball is slightly cupped. It is no use trying to nip right into the cup with a brassie; the ball will not rise far enough to go a considerable distance. But the club in question can be taken if you aim an inch or a little more behind the ball and go through the top roots of the grass.

When the cup is serious, you naturally select an iron club, and then it is a question whether you should cut through the turf behind the ball or "stab" at the ball by coming down on to the back of it just below its center and stopping the club at the impact. It depends on which method you fancy. One thing is certain: If the lie is uphill as well as cuppy, you must stab, because if you try to go through, the rising ground in front will check the club and wreck the shot.

To effect the stab, which is virtually a shot that brings the blade of the iron down between the back of the cup and the ball, and so causes the latter to rise, it is desirable to practice a fairly relaxed grip. You have to make the ball spring up, and you cannot do that if you hold very tightly. It is just at the impact that the grip must ease; prior to that you can hold with the ordinary firmness. If you try the shot, and imbue your mind with the principles of the stab that comes down behind the ball and stops at the impact, you will find that naturally you loosen your wrists as you hit. If you were not to do so, you would break the shaft. Probably it is the subconscious realization of this fact that produces the relaxation.

HOW TO USE THE NIBLICK

Some autobiographical notes

CHAPTER IV

HOW TO USE THE NIBLICK

Some autobiographical notes

THERE IS a method of playing a shot out of a bunker which, in a general sense, is better than any other, but let me straightway warn the golfer against relying upon one manner, and one only, of recovering from places of tribulation on the links. It is an all too common error.

To a large extent every problem under this head has to be considered on its own merits. Much must be governed by the stance which circumstances force the player to adopt, and by the question as to whether he can afford to lose a stroke or ought to make a desperate effort to achieve that which is very difficult. On broad lines, however, it is possible to indicate the right and wrong ways of tackling the average situation in a hazard, and all that I would ask the golfer to remember is that, inasmuch as he has to adapt himself to the needs of the moment, he ought not to depend upon one stereotyped method of executing a bunker shot. As a rule, the position is one that calls for a choice from among several plans of action.

In America the sand in bunkers is usually much harder than it is in Britain. The heat of the sun bakes the soil, and, as a consequence, the ball generally sits up fairly well, whereas at home it sinks into the sand and is often half-buried.

These two sets of conditions call for different tactics. It has been remarked by some critics that when American golfers play in Britain, they do not show so much ability in recovering from bunkers as in the other shots of the game, and the reason is, I suppose, that when they tackle an English or Scottish seaside course, the fine, loose nature of the sand is something new to them. They try to pick the ball up cleanly, which is a sheer impossibility when the bottom of the ball is nestling well down in the sand.

In Britain we have both sets of conditions. The sand is usually hard inland and loose by the sea. When the ball is sitting up on a firm surface, and a good deal of ground has to be covered, the thing to do—unless the position is very close to the face of the hazard—is to hit cleanly. But the shot is not the ordinary lifting one, nor is it a scoop, which is about the worst way imaginable of trying to get out of a bunker. It is a stroke made by addressing the ball with the hands a fraction of an inch in front of it, taking the club up as nearly straight as is humanly possible instead of after the manner of the driving swing, and aiming at the back of the ball—not even a thousandth part of an inch behind it. This principle will make it rise sharply and carry a considerable distance; it is the method adopted by every British professional of note, and it is exactly suited to the conditions which are common in inland bunkers.

"Don't be greedy in a hazard" is perhaps as good a piece of advice as any that can be given in regard to the accomplishment of recovery shots. There are occasions when one has to make a death-or-glory effort, but in ordinary circumstances it is safest, in either a match or a medal round, to look for the easiest way out and trust to making up the lost stroke at a later stage. Most of us have paid the penalty at some time or other of a vaulting ambition to do something wonderful in a bunker.

My unhappiest experience in this respect was in a professional tournament at Musselburgh a good many years ago. At the fourth hole, a short one, I was bunkered near the green. I tried to play a clever shot out with my mashie (very foolishly I carried no niblick in those days), with the result that I took three shots in the hazard. Then I went on to beach, from which place I found my way back into the bunker in which I had had all the trouble.

The hole cost me nine, and I shall never forget the look of withering scorn on the face of my caddie as he said when the ball ultimately went down: "Ye'll have a niblick this afternoon, or I'll no' carry for ye." During the luncheon interval he went off to obtain a niblick. He came back exceedingly intoxicated, but bearing the instrument which he had sworn to make me use. As I was lucky enough to win the tournament in spite of my morning mishap, he felt well repaid for his pains and even perhaps for his aching head on the following morning.

When a ball is lying heavily in sand or other soft substance, then undoubtedly the only way to dislodge it is to aim behind it, so that the club does not actually come into contact with the ball at all, but forces it out of its ensconced position by the violent disturbance of the soil behind the object. This is also a means of escape when the ball is lying cleanly but so near to the face of the hazard that to play it out by direct impact with the club is almost impossible. Here, however, the player will have to be governed by circumstances. It may pay him better in a medal round, or when he has a stroke up his sleeve in a match, to play to the side or even back—anything so long as he makes sure of getting out of the bunker in one stroke.

Everybody who has studied books of instruction knows that the usual advice to a golfer in a bunker is to aim behind the ball, and I am certain that this procedure is often adopted when it is not necessary, as, for instance, when the ball is lying cleanly a yard or two from a fairly shallow face, and can be raised by a firm hit which produces backspin—the stroke which I have described in another chapter. But where the expedient of aiming behind the ball commends itself to the golfer, let him remember to bury the head of the niblick in the sand with all the power that he can command.

It is a very common error to aim behind the ball and then try to carry the club through. This will produce no effect at all, except to move the ball nearer to the face; the whole effort has to finish with the delving of the niblick-head into the sand. How far you aim behind depends upon the distance that you want to make the ball go. If you have only a few yards to travel, you can attack the sand three or four inches behind the ball. It is necessary to keep your vision fixed on that spot, and not to bother about the ball, which will come up all right if you hit with power.

A full swing is wanted, but not a round swing, like that adopted for driving. The movement of the club should be straight up and straight down, or as near to that as you can get.

Sometimes you bring up whole clouds of sand. James Braid plays this and other bunker shots perfectly. I remember it being said that, when he recovered from the bunker at the seventeenth hole at St. Andrews in the Open Championship which he won there in 1905, he made the green tremble by the strength with which he dug into the soil in order to secure a shot of ten yards. At the finish there was almost as much sand outside the hazard as there was in it.

When he and I played a foursome against Duncan and Mayo at about the same period, I deliberately put my partner into the bunker on the left just below the pin at the short sixth hole at Walton Heath in each round. The green was so keen that we were almost certain to be in one or other of the bunkers, and I knew that Braid would put the ball near the hole from this particular hazard. He nearly emptied the bunker of sand, and we won the hole both in the morning and the afternoon.

Perhaps my own best bunker shot was accomplished in this way in a match with Braid. The occasion was the England v. Scotland contest at Sandwich in 1904. We were all square driving from the last tee, and I put my tee shot into the bunker guarding the green. The hole was shorter then than it is now. My ball was dead up against the face of the hazard, twenty yards short of the hole. I took what somebody described as "cartloads of sand," and up came the ball to drop within a few feet of the hole. That shot enabled me to halve the match. If you hit hard enough, and take plenty of sand, you can get the ball out of the most desperate-looking position in a bunker.

Really a more difficult shot is that from long grass. It is no use trying to nip in immediately behind the ball in the hope of executing something in the nature of a stab shot, as many players do. The roots of the grass will always check the pace of the clubhead so effectually as to produce no result worth having.

Neither is an ordinary swing at the ball calculated to achieve the purpose; the club pushes the grass down on the ball and smothers it so completely that it cannot escape. The only way is to aim several inches behind (sometimes as many as four inches), cut right through the roots of the vegetation, and take the ball in the course of the stroke. Naturally, this calls for a shot in which the clubhead travels in one plane for a longer distance than in any other stroke;

it is moving parallel to the ground, and only just clear of it, for five or six inches. But unless you cut through the roots of the grass behind the ball, you will never get that object clear of the entanglement. It is necessary to keep a very firm grip of the club to prevent it turning in the hands.

There are more varieties of long grass in America than in England, and some of them are so stiff that a good deal of strength is required to carve a way through to the ball. Remember not to slow down until the follow-through is well under way; you want to swing as though you were slashing at the grass with a razor and determined to leave the reaper nothing to do in that particular spot.

Above all, never lose your temper when you are in difficulties. Equanimity is half the battle. Some men there are who find it very difficult to remain calm and hopeful in a trying situation. The only thing to do when you see your ball disappear into an unpleasant place is to remember that many a hole is won when it looks lost beyond recall.

I used to know a clergyman who suffered unspeakable agony in his effort to control his feelings when he hit a ball into a bunker. In the graphic words of his caddie: "Big blue pimples would come out on his face and you'd think he was going to have a fit."

THE NIBLICK

ILLUSTRATIVE CHART

STANCE AND ADDRESS.—When playing a niblick shot from a bunker, the stance and address are much the same as for the mashie, with the important exception that the weight of the body must be thrown rather more on the left leg.

BEGINNING OF UPSWING.—The weight of the body has inclined even more on to the left leg. As this is one of the few forcing shots in golf, the club must be held very firmly.

TOP OF SWING.—A decidedly more upright swing than for any other club, on account of the fact that the niblick must be brought down straighter so as to deliver the blow behind the ball instead of taking the latter cleanly off the ground.

In these crises, he always snatched from an inside pocket a prayer book and scurried forward reading it until gradually his rage subsided, and he found himself capable of tackling the situation with a tranquil mind. It must be for everybody to decide how he can best placate himself in such emergencies.

In long grass, one's fancy sometimes turns toward the mashie, but on the whole the niblick is the best club to use when heavy recovery work has to be done. It should be a club with an unbendable shaft and a stout head; it should be the heaviest instrument in the bag and some sixteen or seventeen ounces in weight. Even in the hands of the artist, it is intended for use as something of a bludgeon.

It is a fact—indisputable and inexplicable—that to thousands of golfers the water hazard is the most awe-inspiring on the course.

Many a player who can look a bunker of fearsome proportions straight in the face, take with a brave heart the measure of its sandy expanses, shored up by rugged sleepers, and carry the whole lot as though it were a commonplace accomplishment, has to confess that the sight of a pond or a lake which bars the way to the hole scatters the whole of his confidence.

He feels that he is certain to hit his ball into it. Why he has this fear he does not know. All that he is certain about is that it is vindicated with uncomfortable frequency.

If we could take a pond on a course and any bunker of equal size, and count the number of shots hit into each in a year, we should almost assuredly find the pond an easy winner. By no means is this mysterious attractive power of water peculiar to golf. It is in the nature of things for people to be drawn toward water (except, possibly, as a beverage); that is why they walk to the edge of a lake to inspect it when they would have just as good a view from a distance of thirty yards and why they stand on a bridge or an embankment gazing into a river and yet looking at nothing in particular—except water.

But this fascination is the stronger in golf because, even while the vision is focused on the ball just before the stroke, the pond still lives in the mind's eye. It is something to be avoided, but the picture of it is there all the while, exercising a strange allurement.

If proof were needed of the existence of this influence, it could be found in the novel record which has been established at Garden City, New York—the club that is uppermost in the minds of Britishers when they think of American golf, by reason of the fact that Mr. W. J. Travis, playing as its representative, took the

British amateur championship cup to repose under its roof in 1904. Garden City has—or had—a pond at its last hole, and I understand that club statisticians have calculated the number of balls that enter its clutches in a year. They put the loss down at five thousand balls in twelve months.

A suggestion has been made, I gather, that a net should be laid at the bottom of the pond and drawn up periodically so as to recover the treasure. Trawling might be a good solution to the problem, but it is merely a matter of further arithmetical work to decide how long it will take to fill the pond completely with balls, and thus prevent any others from being sunk. The player would then simply walk on to the expanse of rubber-cored pebbles, and play his ball where it lay—if he could distinguish it.

On British courses a good many ponds have been either drained and converted into bunkers or filled up during recent years. A desire to avert unnecessary loss of balls may have been largely responsible for this tendency, but it is certain that in many places the reason is to be found in the weird enchantment which water exercises on the shots of a considerable proportion of the members.

Be it said that this influence is not confined to the less-practiced golfers. I remember that when I was playing once at Boston, U.S.A., the first thing that caught my eye as I stepped onto the teeing ground was a pond far away to the left.

It was such a long way off that nobody ought to have got into it. And yet I felt somehow that I should be in it. The green could be reached with a cleek, and I kept on telling myself that I must aim well to the right so as not to be near the pond. But, sure enough, my ball went plump into the middle of it. The incident was rather disturbing because the Boston papers had written a lot about my arrival, including interviews which I had never had the honor of supplying. They had come out with big headlines to their columns with the words: "Vardon arrives: Confident of winning and beating record." The first thought that occurred to me as my ball splashed into the pond was the question whether the spectators believed that I had expressed this confidence, and, if so, what their opinion of me was after my first shot.

In the ordinary way, however, it is not so much the distant area of water that attracts the ball as the small pond which is almost under the player's nose—the insignificant pool which he wants to carry with the mashie.

Around London, probably the most imposing water hazard is the lake at the sixteenth hole at Stoke

Poges. The length of the carry depends upon the teeing ground which is in use, but it can be as much as 150 yards, and that affords plenty of scope for error on the part of a moderate golfer who frankly confesses that he hates to be faced by water.

There used to be a jolly old waterman who rowed about that lake recovering balls at a penny a time. Statistics as to his takings in a busy season would have been interesting. He was a lynx-eyed prowler of the deep, with some of the instincts of a diver. He would spot the exact place at which the ball entered the water, and direct his net unerringly to its locale.

The Ranelagh lake, another feature of golf in the English metropolis, also claimed many victims. Even is it said to have in its confines at least one bag of clubs, the property of Mr. Fred Kerr, the actor. One day, when he had driven all his rubbercores, to the number of six, into the lake, he walked dramatically to the water's edge, threw in his clubs, and with the remark, "Old pond, have these as well!" went off home.

The one thing to be said in favor of the water hazard is that it is absolutely impartial. There are no half-measures about its form of punishment; it is a whole-hogger. If both sides get into it, they suffer equally. In ordinary bunkers there is a good deal of luck in the matter of the lie, accentuated by the fact that some players are not so zealous as they should be in smoothing the marks which they make in the sand.

Not long ago I met a golfer who was vowing vengeance on some unknown person who had left a gaping hole in a bunker. My friend had accomplished a particularly low score in the morning, and backed himself at long odds to beat it in the afternoon. He was well on the way to achieving that end, he said, when he came to a short hole near home. His tee shot was bunkered, and when he reached his ball he found it half-buried in a hole as deep as a breakfast cup.

The result was that he took nine strokes in the sand, and twelve to get it down. And, of course, he lost his bet. Probably he lost his temper as well, as I think he must have done, judging by the condition in which I met him. All this would have been avoided if the person who visited the hazard before him had performed his duty to other bunker-users.

No doubt every golfer has suffered the annoyance of getting into somebody else's divot or bunker mark. It might not be a bad idea to make it the honorable obligation of a partner or opponent to draw attention to his companion's delinquencies in forgetting to repair the scarred earth.

I daresay that it often happens that the golfer

blames the heel mark in the bunker when none actually exists. Most of us have witnessed unfortunate heroes hammering away in places of retribution for so long a period as to suggest the possibility of their having acquired a lease of the unhappy spot, just as some morbidly disposed individuals like to live in houses in which murders have been committed. When this type of golfer does at length emerge from the hazard, he generally says that his ball was buried in a hole made by somebody else. On a London course I once saw a player make a drive from the first tee which landed in a pot bunker on the left. He entered this simple-looking resort of the erring, and to the people who were awaiting his pleasure, it seemed to be an age before he came out again.

He worked his way round and round the walls of his prison, ever hitting the ball and never quite extricating it. He was like a bird of the forest suddenly trapped and fluttering its wings with feverish excitement at the bars of its gaol in a frenzied effort to regain its freedom. At the finish, he explained that he was in a deep heel mark. Judging by the time he spent in getting out, he must have been in something like a coal mine.

In the ordinary way there is little excuse for anybody taking more than one shot in a hazard. I suppose that, in the majority of instances, it is either lack of forethought or excess of ambition that leads to disaster in bunkers. Except where the ball lies in an obviously hopeless position, the temptation to attempt a tour de force is nowhere stronger than in a hazard. Yet the lesson that is learned by studying the doings of successful players is that, unless the lie is particularly favorable, it is sound policy to resign oneself on the spot to the loss of a stroke as punishment for a mistake, and to trust to recovering it later.

A long shot from a hazard is a thrilling piece of self-satisfaction and a fine spectacle. The wise man is he who tries it only when it can be done, and that is not often. Just once in a while you see the chance of bringing it off. Almost my last personal experience of it was on a Brighton course. The ball was lying on the sloping face of a bunker, and it had to come up quickly in order to escape the top. Fortunately, the face of the hazard was by no means precipitous, and with a brassie I managed to get the ball away and deposit it on the green, two hundred yards ahead.

At Prestwick, in the British Open Championship of 1914, (J. H.) Taylor took his brassie in a bunker at the ninth hole and hit almost as long a shot as he would have accomplished from the fairway. That sort of thing is possible on occasion, and certain it is that it is considerably easier to the crack golfer who is tolerably sure of controlling the elevation of the ball than to the mediocre player, whose every shot is a dash into the great unknown. Yet the latter is far more disposed than the top-sawyer to essay a long shot from a bunker.

In point of fact, it is comparatively seldom that one sees a first-class performer obtain considerable distance from a hazard. Very often his restraint must seem disappointing. He merely howks the ball out, twenty or thirty or forty yards up the course. Yet it is not always that a shot of hair-raising brilliancy is outside the range of possibility. It is simply that in normal circumstances the effort is not worth the risk that it involves.

When there is no alternative to a death-or-glory endeavor, people sometimes do amazing things. One of the best bunker shots I have ever seen was that by Edward Ray when, in the final of the News of the World tournament at Walton Heath in 1911, his chance seemed gone beyond recall. Standing two down with three to go, Ray was about as badly bunkered at the sixteenth hole as any but the most cruel-hearted person could conceive. His ball was lying half-buried close to the face of a hazard three feet high, with the green one hundred yards ahead.

By making the ball rise quickly, aiming to the left so as to give it a chance to get up before reaching the face of the bunker, and imparting a tremendous amount of slice to the shot, he actually got onto the green and halved in four. Most of the people had walked away, convinced that he could not possibly prolong the match.

That, however, was a desperate situation which called for a desperate endeavor. In the ordinary way I would say to the club golfer, "Look for the easiest way out, and concentrate on escaping from the hazard in one shot."

There are times when there is nothing for it but to trust to one's instinct and adaptability to secure the best possible position for playing an unusual shot. I remember on one occasion at Muirfield having to go down on to both knees in order to get at a ball which was lying close up to the deep face of a bunker running parallel with the course. In this case, however, perhaps it would have been better if I had stood in the bunker and recovered by playing back. Sometimes, in a hazard, it is worthwhile remembering that one is entitled to retrace one's steps; nobody likes it, but occasionally it is the easiest and safest way out of trouble, especially when there is a good chance of reaching the green with the next shot.

A ditch is another painful place of retribution. You may have to stand with one foot in it and one out, or in some other uncomfortable way. There is only one golden rule to observe when the ball is badly in a ditch; it is to bring the niblick down with a crash about an inch behind the object—just as one does in the sand when particularly horribly bunkered—so that the upheaval of soil will make the ball jump up and escape. Unless you have plenty of room in which to swing and the chance of making the ball fly straight—a privilege that is not often forthcoming in a ditch—it is not much use trying to take the ball cleanly.

We have reached the end of lessons. I hope that, here and there, the hints that I have given may be helpful to the golfer who, loving the game as a hobby and a recreation, wants to play it well. More than any other pastime that I know—and I have tried most forms of sport—does it fan the flames of emulation. I doubt whether anywhere there is a golfer of any age who does not hope to do better tomorrow than he did today, though this afternoon he played the round of his life. His ambition is ever upward.

Sometimes it is said that success on the links is impossible to the person who has neglected the game in his or her early youth. I am not so sure of that. The value of a training in schooldays is unquestionable; but it is possible to make up for a great deal of lost time if you set about the task in the right way—the way that I have endeavored to indicate.

I have just expressed that sentiment aloud, and somebody has said, "What about yourself? You must have been playing every day when you were a boy." I most certainly wasn't playing anything like every day, or even once a week, when I was a boy. It is a very good thing for a youngster to learn the swing at the time when the imitative faculty of the young mind is at its best; but I am sure that an exaggerated importance is attributed to the assiduous pursuit of the game in childhood.

I realize that, in saying this, I am guilty of something akin to heresy. It is customary in discussing the beginnings of famous golfers to produce evidence that, as soon as they could toddle they went out and practiced with a diligence worthy of veterans. We have been told repeatedly how they stuck to the game through their teens, until at length they could be said to have grown up with it—the only way, according to tradition, to master golf.

So many people have told us that the one royal road to success is to take up the game in childhood and play it until it becomes ingrained in the constitution—to be "teethed on a golf-club handle," as it has been put—that I see no reason to withhold evidence to the contrary with a piece of autobiography.

Up to the time I was twenty years of age, I played so little golf that even now I can remember almost every round as a red-letter event of my youthful days. We were a big family of six boys and two girls, and at the age of twelve I went out to work to do my bit in the maintenance of the home. At that time I had not the slightest thought of taking seriously to golf. To be sure, the formation of the Royal Jersey Golf Club five years previously, at our little village of Grouville, had prompted most of the boys in the village to dabble in the game. We had a little course of our own, and some homemade clubs of a primitive kind, in which a stick from a blackthorn served as the shaft and a piece of oak as the head, the two being fastened together by boring a hole in the "head" with a red-hot poker, inserting the blackthorn stick and tightening the joint with the aid of wedges. Of iron clubs we had none.

Truth to tell, however, I was not particularly keen on the game, and played very seldom. I used to busy myself at the beach, collecting seaweed which sold for a sum that brought a nice few pounds a year into the family exchequer. I think that, whatever may have been my faults, I can claim to have been a boy who wasted little time. One of my little passions was to collect all the nails I could find by extracting them from discarded pieces of wood, straightening them with a hammer when they were bent, and assembling them in a box which I had made with eight compartments for the different sizes of nails. I obtained a truly imposing array, and was glad to learn from my mother, a few years ago, that she was still keeping the box of nails that came of my boyish idea of industrial economy.

When I was thirteen, I entered a doctor's service to act as page-boy and wait at table. For four years I had virtually no golf at all. To be sure, I would go out occasionally with other boys on moonlight nights for a game, but I do not know that my spasmodic appearances on the links in these circumstances can be held to have constituted very serious practice. In later days people often said to me, "I used to know you when you were playing golf as a boy at Jersey." In point of fact, it was my brother Tom they knew, for he obtained a good deal of golf, whereas I was not far from being a stranger to the game. Apart from my duties as page-boy, I helped to make butter and performed various other duties, so that there was not much time for golf.

When I was seventeen, I went as gardener to Major Spofforth—a brother of Mr. F. R. Spofforth, the famous Australian cricketer, who was known in two hemispheres as "the demon bowler." Major Spofforth was keen on golf, and every now and again he took me out to play. He also gave me some of his old clubs, which seemed very wonderful after the clumsy, homemade things that I had been using. All the same, I was not at this period a diligent seeker of success on the links. I liked cricket and football, and went in a good deal for running, winning ten prizes as a sprinter. I remember, during a holiday, taking part in six races in two days.

One of my duties was to scare the crows from an area of ground under cultivation, and to render the job as interesting as possible, I made a practice of playing an improvised kind of golf around the field. I had my own marks that ranked as holes and was always trying to beat my own "record"—it was my own because nobody else ever attacked it. No doubt this experience was useful, although I never regarded it as anything but a means of relieving the dullness of a slow job.

Apart from an occasional round with Major Spofforth—which invariably made me feel very nervous—my golf was limited to Christmas, Easter, Whitsun, and August Bank Holiday. On these occasions I played mostly with Willie Gaudin, who subsequently went to America. Major Spofforth once said to me, "Henry, if I were you I would not give up my golf; it may be useful to you some day." I remembered the words, but at that time I had not the remotest idea of developing into a champion.

My first attempt to play golf in a really earnest frame of mind was when, at the age of twenty, I entered a competition for a vase given by the local working men's club. We had to play one round a month for six months, and I won pretty easily. Alas! the prize—my most cherished trophy because it was my first, although it had no great monetary value—was destroyed when a German airman dropped a bomb at the back door of my home at Totteridge and brought the building tumbling about the ears of myself and my family.

Just before my first competition concluded, the news reached me that my brother Tom, who had gone to England to launch out as a professional golfer, had won second prize in an open professional tournament at Musselburgh. The award was twenty pounds. It seemed an enormous amount to me, and I pondered long and intently over it. I knew that, little as I had played, I was as good as Tom. If he could win that vast fortune, why shouldn't I?

My father—himself a golfer—was not enamored of my ambition to become a professional. He had never seen me play; there had been very few opportunities for him to do so. It was not until I had won three championships that he saw my golf for the first time.

He had watched Tom on a good many occasions and was satisfied that he would make a golfer, but he could not reconcile himself to the belief that a person who took such a dilettantish interest in the game as myself would ever excel at it. Happy and sacred his memory! Even in later years he declined to abandon his early convictions and was wont to say, "Harry wins the prizes, but Tom plays the golf."

I have said enough to show that a boy need not grow up from babyhood "teethed on a golf-club handle" and play the game diligently in his young days in order to excel at it.

If I had a son, I would not attempt to force the golfing pace upon him. Until he attained at least the age of fourteen, I would tell him simply to watch good players and to copy them. Children cannot be taught golf, but they are born mimics, and if you put them into good company they will grow up in the right way. You must let them do as they will for a time—at any rate on the links—and then when they rise to such discretion as the age of fourteen or fifteen engenders in them, you can give them hints that will make them advance rapidly.

At home, I studied the styles of the golfers I saw because it seemed natural to do so, but I cannot say that I molded my methods on those of anybody in particular. I never had a lesson, and cannot recall anybody who impressed me as being a model who should be copied.

There is some mystery about the consistency with which the Jersey golfers have adapted themselves to the upright swing—that compact manner of wielding the club which came as a shock to the people who for years had worshipped the longer and flatter method known as the St. Andrews swing. My own brother and Edward Ray, the Gaudins, the Becks, and the Renoufs, all drifted involuntarily into the habit of taking the club to the top of the swing by the shortest route, whereas the popular way before was to sweep the club back flat at the start and make a very full flourish of the swing. Why we hit upon the other way we do not know.

Personally, I never thought about the matter until I obtained my first professional post at Ripon, Yorkshire. And it was when I was twenty-one and in my second appointment at Bury, Lancashire, that I began to study and learn golf in real earnest.

HOW TO USE THE MASHIE

*With hints on practicing
and some adventures*

CHAPTER V

HOW TO USE THE MASHIE

*With hints on practicing
and some adventures*

THE MASHIE shot in golf is a specialized shot. In its main features it is a law unto itself.

I have heard people say that the swing for every club in the bag is the same. They declare that the differences which present themselves to the eye in a first-class player's way of managing his set of implements—his less upright and more upright swings, according to the club that is in use, and the effects of those swings on the flight of the ball—are merely the results of variations in the lengths and lofts of the clubs.

I do not desire to criticize that judgment at all severely. Once you know the correct swing for driving, you are on a very fair way to mastering all the shots in the game, and I agree that, when using the cleek, midiron, and kindred clubs for plain straightforward shots, you need not be conscious of attempting anything very different from that which you essayed with the driver. Such changes as are desirable

119

are matters of stance rather than swing, as I have explained in the chapters concerning those clubs.

When you take in hand the mashie, I do not suggest for a moment that you should blot out your prevailing idea of the swing and try to substitute another. But what I do say is that it is a specialized shot that you make with the mashie; that if the swing is the same, only on a smaller scale, as with the clubs of longer range, you are never so safe as when you produce that swing in a way specially adapted to the club.

I am assuming that you do not take full bangs with the mashie, like a slogger at cricket making a death-or-glory swipe at the ball in the hope of carrying not only the fieldsmen and the spectators but the pavilion as well. Some golfers do that, but it is not the mashie's work. It is a club built for calculated approaching. It is meant above all things to control the flight of the ball so that when you are within ready hail of the putting green—certainly little, if any, more than one hundred yards from it—you can play the ball with that feeling that the mashie ought to give of being able to bring the ball to rest within holing distance. You cannot have much of that feeling when you are hitting with what somebody has described as divine frenzy. You can only trust to luck in those circumstances.

The way to cultivate a sense of assurance with the mashie is to have the club under restraint all the while; to know that you can get the distance without forcing. And the way to keep the mashie under complete control is to work the hip-pivot of the body—for we must turn the body at the hips for every shot except a putt—from the knees instead of from the feet. Let the feet be so steadily established on the ground that you lift the left heel hardly at all as you take the club back, and the right heel hardly at all as you finish. Let the feet—which in longer shots have played an important part in the winding-up and unwinding of the body—be merely agents for supporting the working of the knees.

First of all, we must stand properly. The stance should be decidedly open; that is to say, the body should be facing more toward the hole than for iron shots. Have the ball opposite the left heel and about twenty inches distant from it, with the toes of the foot pointing well outward. Let the right foot be square to the line that you propose to take, and put it so far forward that the toes, pointing straight ahead, are a good eight inches ahead of the toes of the left foot pointing outward. Thus we are standing well over the ball, with the body facing distinctly toward the hole.

The secret of the successful mashie swing is to

inaugurate the turn of the body from the knees so
that the feet remain almost motionless from beginning to end. The posture should be one of relaxation
with an element of slackness at the knees. As in all
other shots, the club starts first. With the mashie the
body does not screw around so far as when clubs of
longer range are in use, but it must turn a little at the
hips to prevent swaying. As it thus turns the right leg
stiffens until it is straight. When it is in that condition
the upswing is complete. Meanwhile, the left knee
will have bent slightly. It must have done so if you
have remembered to keep the foot practically station-
ary—or, at any rate, not to have lifted the heel very
much from the ground.

The downswing is a matter of unscrewing the
body by returning the right knee to its original bent
position. In short, then, you obtain the turn of the
hips by stiffening the right knee and bending the left,
and then stiffening the left and bending the right.
The knees control the whole action of the body as it
follows the arms and the club. As the club goes
through you can raise the outer side of the right foot
from the ground so as to be resting on the inner side,
but do not lift the heel if you can help it. What many
players do is to make free with both feet, and so lose
the stability of stance which helps in accurate hitting.

Keep your head down and still until the ball has been struck, and do not attempt to work the wrists in an attempt to scoop the ball into the air. The club will lift it all right (it is shaped for that purpose) if you simply aim half an inch behind the ball and play straight through it. If you want a lot of loft, take the niblick. It is a pretty sound rule that endeavoring to shovel the ball into the air by a turn of the wrists is sure to end in disaster. The body should not move either back during the upswing or forward at the finish. It is quite enough for it to turn at the hips through the action of the knees. The club will look after the ball.

Very many golfers take almost a full swing with the mashie and then try to come down slowly so as to hit at the requisite strength. That is entirely wrong. If you were knocking a stone with a stick, you would strike it smartly; you would not deliberate about the pace of the stick. So, with the mashie, you must always come down smartly. There must be no faltering. In a sense, you hit as firmly as when you are driving. The only difference is that if you do not take the club up far, you have not time to get the same pace on the club as when executing a full swing, and so the impact is less powerful. The tendency to try and scoop the ball into the air is strongest when you are near the hole. Some players then lay the blade of the club right back or else poke it under the ball as they hit; they feel that they must make some special effort to be sure of lifting the object. This fancy work is the cause of half the foozling.

To overcome the habit I recommend my pupils to practice pitching over a bush, starting at seventy yards and gradually reducing the distance to twenty yards. At seventy yards you are compelled to hit firmly, without any attempt at scooping, in order to obtain the necessary carry. If you play three shots at that range, then three at sixty yards, then three at fifty yards, and so on down to twenty yards, and always play them in the same way except that you shorten the upswing as you draw nearer to the bush, you ought to get out of the fatal way of trying to shovel the ball into the air by a turn of the wrists. The best distance at which to practice with the mashie is from forty to sixty yards. Personally, for an ordinary pitch-and-run shot, I generally play for a spot about three yards short of the hole. If the ball strikes a piece of ground of average firmness, it will run to somewhere near the hole. Of course, if it pitches on soft turf it will stop short, and if it lands on a very hard piece it will run past. That cannot be helped.

It is good occasionally to practice pitching with

the niblick, which is a useful club when you want the ball to rise quickly and stop almost where it pitches. Its disadvantage compared with the mashie is that the edge of its sole is very sharp and is therefore apt to stick into the ground and spoil the stroke unless you play it perfectly. Still, it is a very valuable alternative for the person who is not proficient at the cut stroke with the mashie, which is one of the most difficult shots in the game.

I played the best stroke of my life with a niblick. It was in a tournament at Northwood, near London, when my ball lay within four feet of the clubhouse—a building thirty feet high, which barred the way to the green about thirty yards ahead in a straight line. To tell the truth, I don't know quite how it was done—I only know that I applied more backspin than ever I got on any other shot and hit with all my might. Spectators will vouch for the fact that the ball rose almost straight till it reached the top of the clubhouse and then sailed forward and stopped a yard from the pin. After which I missed the putt! That brought me to my senses.

Approaching with the mashie or the niblick—and in all save a few circumstances I recommend the mashie, because it is really the easier club to use, even at short range—is, I suppose, the most popular of all forms of golf practice. There is a fascination in trying to place the ball near an objective, whether it be a mark on the fairway or a flag-pin in a putting green. Personally, I never tire of it. Often I engage in it when waiting five minutes for a pupil, and much as it is pursued, I do not think that the average golfer has enough of it.

Many an odd quarter of an hour would be well spent in practicing mashie shots with half a dozen balls—first from about ninety yards and then from fifty yards. If you choose your training pitch wisely, you are in no danger of losing your treasured rubbercores. You can see exactly where they alight; retrieve them in two or three minutes; and start again. When I was younger I practiced matching one ball against another in mashie pitches. It taught my hand and eye a lot.

Success in approaching is largely a matter of practice—not of physical attributes nor an inborn capacity for playing games. Indeed, I would go further and say that where the average golfer has the best opportunity of making progress is in the mashie shot—the shot of one hundred yards or less.

Willie Park once said that "the man who can putt is a match for anybody," to which the obvious retort was that "the man who can approach has no need to be able to putt." The pitch-and-run mashie shot is really a simple operation, and that four golfers out of five play it badly is due to the fact that they do too much fanciful pivoting and wristwork when actually only the plainest of plain movements is required. They think it is difficult, and therefore make it difficult.

If you can approach well, you will win far more matches than ever you will lose. I have some particularly joyous memories of the usefulness of deadly approaching, and none more happy than that of a match which I played with an English Internationalist, Tom Williamson, on a nine-hole course at Radcliffe-on-Trent, some years ago. Each of us was immensely keen on winning, because, on the night preceding the contest, we were shown a handsome cup which a member of the club had presented as a reward for the victor. It was a course that exactly suited the man who could drive and pitch. The holes were neither short nor long; at most of them, after a good tee shot, you wanted a mashie. I was up betimes (early) next morning practicing with that club, and I think I used it as well as need be. My scores for three rounds of the nine holes were 31, 32, and 31. I won by 11 up and 9 to play. There were three 2's in the afternoon, in connection with which the mashie took a perhaps inordinate part, since it sent the ball into the hole. I holed very few putts of more than three or four yards.

Williamson's father, who used to be a station-master nearby (he was very keen on golf, and it was funny to see him playing in the regalia of gold-braided cap and uniform and dodging into the gorse when a train went by in case he should be seen by an official in it), was very cut up about the result. When a late arrival asked him the result, he replied: "Tom didn't turn up; at least, I don't think anybody saw him."

That, at any rate, shows you what mashie-approaching can do, because, on that occasion, neither my driving nor my putting was out of the ordinary. Where most golfers make mistakes with the mashie is that they pivot too much on their feet, try to scoop the ball into the air instead of letting the loft of the club do the work for which it was built, and throw their weight forward at the impact, at the same time raising their heads to see the result of the shot. Many, too, take almost a full swing and endeavor to regulate the pace of the club coming down—a thing nobody could do with consistent success. In short, they make a big and intricate job of what is truly a simple matter. Possibly it is the very simplicity of which they are suspicious; they think there must be more in it than meets the eye. There isn't.

I have mentioned the importance of practicing,

THE MASHIE

ILLUSTRATIVE CHART

STANCE AND ADDRESS.—Note that the player is closer to the ball than for any former shot, and the body is bending so that the head is well over the ball. The position is one of ease—no tautness of the muscles.

BEGINNING OF UPSWING.—The chief movement has been the bending of the left knee, in order to cause the hip to pivot. This pivoting has really begun at the knee and the left heel has hardly risen from the ground.

TOP OF SWING.—The left knee has bent a little more, and the heel is just off the ground. This length of swing is little more than a half-swing and is as much as the good golfer attempts with the mashie, because of the vital need for controlling the length of the shot.

and a few hints as to the best way to go about it in all its phases may not be out of place at this stage.

It is a rather curious fact that the value of practice is realized far less by the moderate golfer than by the crack player. Often you will hear an inveterate foozler say to a champion:

"If I could play like you, I wouldn't practice as you do; I'd prefer a match every time."

What is more, the long handicap man is not easily to be persuaded into going out for an hour to a quiet corner of the course and studying in solitude the questions of cause and effect. Always must he have a rival. That is one of the reasons why he retains a long handicap. One is so keen in a match or a medal round that it is impossible to do all the thinking—or, at any rate, the kind of thinking—that leads to efficiency.

No matter what the grade of the golfer, practice is valuable to him. Never can he be so good a player that it is impossible for him to be better. Personally, I have made it a rule to practice "on my own" at frequent intervals all my life, and I am certain that every successful golfer has done the same. Man for man, or woman for woman, there is infinitely more devotion to this subject among advanced players than there is where the less-accomplished performers are concerned. That is precisely why the former are advanced.

The trouble is to make the less accomplished appreciate the importance of a lonely hour on the links.

For a beginner or a foozler of long standing, nothing could be better than an hour's practice every day
for a month and an entire abstinence from competi-
tive rounds. I know that it is a lot to ask of a person
who is longing to prove his progress and prowess by
conquering somebody, but it is the surest means of
economizing on the links in time and money that was
ever conceived. It is the only way to learn the things
that the professional has taught.

The player who goes straight out and expects to put
the hints into operation as though he had only to hear
them in order to master them is not likely to profit
greatly by his lessons. By the time he reaches the
fourth hole he forgets nearly everything in his anxiety
to do something better than his opponent. In my early
days as a professional, I devoted practically a year to
practice. That was when I was at Ripon, in Yorkshire—
my first engagement, entered upon at the age of twenty. Perhaps I was lucky in the fact that there were so
few players in those days that the opportunity of a
match rarely presented itself, and so there was nothing
to do but practice or else exchange my clubs for the
gamekeeper's gun and go rabbit-shooting while he
tried to do holes in anything from four to forty.

In any case, it was during that year that I learned most of my golf, including the overlapping grip, the low-flying backspin shot with an iron club, and the other ideas that were useful in a later period. Until I went to Ripon I had made very little study of the game. I had played it, as most people do, for the fun of the thing, and engaged almost entirely in matches and competitions. I can say with perfect truth that I never had a lesson from anybody (there was nobody to give me one), but I was a very much better golfer when I left Ripon, after a year, than when I went there. Such was the result of practice, and its effects I remember with gratitude.

What I would recommend the aspiring golfer to do is to go out at the start with a brassie and iron. He can leave the mashie till later. We will assume that he is going to devote an hour to the business in hand. Let him proceed to a remote part of the course, where he will not be flurried by passing couples, and play tee shots with his brassie for fifteen minutes, then iron shots from the turf for fifteen minutes, and repeat the process. He will find it convenient to have a dozen balls, and a caddie to make the tee for the brassie-drives and collect the balls when they have been dispatched, but this is a matter for personal consideration.

The main point is that this system of practicing without having to bother about an opponent's shot cultivates the gift of concentration, and enables the player to reflect upon the lessons that he has learned and to try and fathom the causes of his failure if he is not executing the strokes satisfactorily.

Thus, if he slices three drives in succession, he sets himself to find out the reason—a thing he has little time to do in a match. I have explained previously that I advise a brassie for the moderate golfer's tee shots when he is practicing, because its loft and stiffness of shaft render it easier to use than a driver, and the confidence thus gained will not be lost when he comes to take the strictly correct club.

If the temperament of the student be such that he cannot stand a whole hour with two clubs, he had better include a mashie and a putter in his practicing kit, and allot ten minutes to drive, ten minutes to iron shots, ten minutes to pitching, ten minutes to putting, and then a further ten minutes each to drives and iron strokes. These are the shots on which to concentrate at the outset. I do not believe in more than an hour's practice at a time. At the end of that period the player is apt to become a trifle weary of the proceedings, and to continue in that condition is to do more harm than good. I have read that Mr. Walter

J. Travis used to give an hour to each club and practice for hours on end. Some people may be able to do
that without suffering a sense of boredom, but it
would not suit the average individual. You must
retain a very live and keen interest in what you are
doing. If you can manage it, there is much to be said
for the scheme of practicing for an hour in the morning and an hour in the evening. The day's break
brings you zestfully to the evening session.

There is no harm occasionally in playing a hole
on your own. What I used to do frequently was to take
a couple of balls and play them against one another.
I still do that occasionally, especially when I am
preparing on my home course for an important
event, and there is really quite a lot of fun in it, with
the added recommendation of usefulness. You concentrate equally on the shots since it is not a matter
of being beaten by somebody, and at each hole you
get two drives, two irons or pitches, and all the putts
that fate may prompt you to take.

I used to play nine holes in this way, and I found
that if I got two or three up on myself, the resolution
with which my worse half would set about the task of
retrieving the situation was such as to keep me
intensely interested all the while.

It is not necessary, however, to go to the lengths of

a player whom I knew and who favored this system of practicing to such an extent that he used to take out two bags of clubs (and carry them himself), go the whole round of the course, and consider that each bag represented a player. One was a new set of clubs and the other an old set, and he would no more have thought of borrowing from the new when the old was due to play, or vice versa, than of cheating himself about the scores for the respective holes. He was a regular Jerkily and Hide of the links, and he got on very well, as surely he deserved to do.

Be it said that one can learn much as to the clubs that are suitable in these periods of solitary practice. That is a point to which I have always paid close attention in the weeks preceding championships, and as the result of my experiments, important changes have sometimes taken place in my equipment. Thus, just before the big events of 1914, I found that my driver of long acquaintance had lost its charm. Rummaging about in the shop, I came across a driver that had been discarded a year earlier because it seemed to be too light. I fancied it now and decided to try it against the other. The discovery won, and it helped me considerably to win the British Open Championship and other events of that season.

Prior to an important occasion, the wise aspirant

to success goes thoroughly into the question of his kit and his capabilities in various departments of the game, because he knows that if he leaves everything till the eleventh hour, when he has reached the scene of action he will not be able to make changes and try experiments in the same peace of mind as on his own course. That is why you see a crack golfer practicing so often. The moderate player may urge that no occasion is especially important to him, and that, therefore, he lacks the incentive to devote time regularly to practice. But we may assume that he wants to improve, and I am sure that the best way to do it is the way that champions have found profitable.

I do not believe the man who says he plays only for exercise and that he does not care whether his form is good or bad. As a rule, he makes such a remark when he is about five down at the turn. Golf is a pastime that compels a person to want to do better than ever he has done in the past. Its nature is to open up wonderful possibilities and generate inexhaustible hope. And so the player is always believing in his power to improve.

Home exercises of the dumbbell and Indian club variety, such as a good many golfers make a habit of performing with a view to strengthening their arms and wrists, are not necessary. Indeed, sometimes they are positively harmful from a golfing point of view, since they may develop strength of muscle as opposed to what I would call a healthy and normal suppleness. Golf is essentially a natural game; a man needs to be fit in order to play it well, and it keeps him fit, but he does not want abnormal muscular development. If you have a room sufficiently large, it is not a bad idea to practice some swings on the days when you cannot visit the course. This process helps to keep the arms and shoulders in working order. For the same reason, the indoor schools that are so numerous in America are useful in the winter, although it is not possible to tell when hitting a ball into a net quite what would have happened to it if its flight had not been arrested.

For the player who desires to advance, I recommend at least three hours' practice every week, and in the interests of the golfing community, it may be suggested that these outings should have their base somewhere near the edge of the fairway instead of in the middle. They are apt to result in the lifting of a good many divots, some of them very large if the player is in his novitiate.

I once saw a beginner at Totteridge miss the ball completely and yet lose it. He slogged blindly with an iron and lifted a piece of turf about as big as a soup plate. The divot dropped neatly on the ball just in front. Not seeing the latter object, the player thought he had hit it. "Where's it gone?" he asked excitedly. It was not until somebody told him to replace the divot that he found it had not gone at all.

After lessons, we are entitled to turn to lighter entertainment. It has been suggested that somewhere in this work I should describe some of the odd experiences that have befallen me on the links. We have been serious so long that why should I not do it here?

Far more than any other game does golf lend itself to the provision of strange incidents and exciting little adventures. It is played in a setting of nature; its home is on the open moorland or the rolling links by the sea; there is much in it that appeals to the primeval instincts of man because of the unrestraint of its environment.

I hesitate to believe the story which Andrew Kirkaldy told us when he came back from Mexico that it was a common thing to be confronted at a lonely part of the course by a bandit who suddenly emerged from a wood and with the command, supported by a six-shooter: "Hands up! Your money or your life!" proceed to rob the match of all its valuables. But we have all read with bated breath of the perils which are encountered by enthusiasts in some countries, where savage beasts of the forest are among the "agencies outside the match," and death-dealing snakes are said sometimes to be found coiled up in the holes. I am glad to say I have not yet been subjected to the trial of playing a game amid such distractions, but in England I have had one engagement with an animal which I shall not readily forget, and which gave me a very anxious five minutes.

The episode occurred when I was professional to the Bury Club, Lancashire, something like thirty years ago. In those days golf eked out a rather precarious existence in England. The landlord of the ground on which our course was situated had no respect at all for the people who came to hit a ball about his estate. We were there on sufferance, and one of the troubles that we had to endure was that he insisted on putting his prize bulls to graze on the course. They were a fine collection of animals, and one—a white bull—had secured for him many prizes, but they made a round of golf a risky proceeding, and there were many players who would not venture so far as the first tee when these bovine hazards were in evidence.

The white bull was particularly ill-disposed toward us. Often it sent us scuttling to places of safety when, just as we were preparing to accomplish a critical shot, we saw it galloping toward us, with eyes

ablaze and tail whirling ferociously in the air. I had
to make several hasty and undignified flights in consequence of its unruliness; but whenever anybody
complained to the landlord about its behavior, he
invariably said: "You shouldn't tease him. He would
be all right if you'd leave him alone."

One day I decided upon what seemed to me to be
a fine plan. Our putting greens were surrounded by
wire, so as to protect them from invasion by the animals. After about the fiftieth of my retreats from the
white bull, I told the owner that if ever it went for me
again, I should enter one of those protected areas,
wait for the animal to come up to the wire, and then
stick it in a vital part with the flag-pin which was in
the hole. The flag-pin struck me as being a splendid
idea; already I saw myself in the role of toreador.

"Don't tease the thing," he said again, "and you
won't have any trouble with it."

Not long afterward, I was inspecting the course in
connection with the work of its upkeep, when I saw
the bull approaching me in its usual truculent mood.
It was fast gathering pace, so I made a dash for a putting green, leapt over the wire, seized the flag-pin,
and returned to the fortification to carry out my
stern resolve. On came the bull until it reached the
bulwark—and then, to my horrified astonishment, it

calmly put its feet over the wire and was in the enclo-
sure with me.

I jumped out again, and fortunately retained sufficient self-possession to realize that in the open field
it would be no use trying to outpace the animal. I
started to run around the wire on the outside, where-
upon the bull followed me on the inside. Round and
round we went, I know not how many times.

Every now and again the enemy made a dash at
me, but the wire kept him back, and luckily for me it
never occurred to him to come out as he had entered.
I realized, however, that if I ran away or stopped still,
he would be over in an instant.

Which of us would have collapsed first I do not
know. The question was never put to the test, thanks
to the providential intervention of a muffin-man. On
a road about a hundred yards away this muffin-man
approached, ringing his bell. Directly the bull heard
the tinkle, it set off pell-mell in the direction of my
innocent deliverer. A hedge on the fringe of the thor-
oughfare barred its progress, and meanwhile I fled to
a place of safety.

There was a rather interesting sequel to this incident. One day I was relaying a teeing ground close to
the fowl-house, which graced the course. In the midst
of the work my attention was suddenly diverted by the

spectacle of the white bull chasing its owner. He was running like a madman, and evidently in a state of panic, and in his desperation he dashed into the middle of the duckpond near the fowl-house, where he stood almost up to his neck in water. I have to confess at this moment I was so unsympathetic as to shout: "You shouldn't tease the animal. He'd be all right if you'd leave him alone."

The bull rushed up to the edge of the pond, where he stood lashing his tail angrily and glaring fiercely at his master. Then followed one of the pluckiest deeds that I have ever seen done by a boy. The landlord's son, a youth of about ten, seized the animal by the tail, and tried to pull him away. The bull turned around several times in savage efforts to get at the boy, but he held on like grim death. All of an instant the animal set off at top pace for its shed, dragging its assailant at its heels, and a few minutes later it was safely inside. The owner was so enraged that he followed it in and killed it by sticking it with a four-pronged fork, and that was the end of our troubles with the white bull of Bury.

Such was a sample of the conditions under which we pursued golf in England in those unsophisticated days when the game attracted little attention and when the expenditure of large sums of money on the provision of comfort was considered unnecessary. I love to recall my associations with Bury, where I spent one of the happiest times of my life, but I cannot imagine what the modern golfer would think of the circumstances under which we played the game there. On summer evenings the famous Besses-o'-the-Barn Band, which has performed in all parts of the world, had the special right to use our last putting green as a place for practicing. Fancy an up-to-date club permitting one of its treasured and carefully nurtured greens to be converted into a bandstand!

Caddies provide some of the richest humor of the links, and it is a pity that the stories of them are so often spoilt in print by the impossibility of conveying the quaint air of equality which so many of these club-bearers (and generally the best of them) adopt in their attitude toward their employers.

"Big" Crawford, perhaps the most famous of all the North Berwick caddies, was a real character. Many tales of him have been published; here is one which, I think, is not generally known.

For some time prior to his death, Crawford kept the ginger-beer hut at the far end of the North Berwick links, and on special occasions he made a point of hoisting a flag over the structure. The Grand Duke Michael of Russia, paying one of his periodical visits to the course, duly reached the hut, and was evidently gratified to see the sign of rejoicing.

"It's very good of you, Crawford," he said, "to have your flag out for me."

"Na, na, Mr. Michael," replied Crawford (he always called the Grand Duke "Mr." Michael), "it's for a better man than you. It's for Mr. Balfour." His admiration of Mr. Balfour was intense, and I believe that the latter, when writing to engage his favorite caddie, invariably began the letter, "My dear Crawford."

I had one personal experience of Crawford. In 1899 I went to North Berwick to play the first half of my match with Willie Park—the event which I regard as the most important of my golfing career. It was so because it provoked discussion for nearly a year before it took place (we were a long time coming to terms), and I do not think that two men ever embarked on a contest with a more desperate desire to win.

On the evening before the beginning of the match, I went for a walk with my brother Tom. Suddenly "Big" Crawford appeared around a corner, and like a flash he hurled a huge horseshoe at me.

If I had not dodged it would have struck me on the head, and at the pace at which it was traveling it would very nearly have brained me. Truth to tell, I did not altogether appreciate this method of delivering good fortune, but it was impossible to do other than laugh when he explained that he had put every penny he possessed on me and was determined to bring me luck.

There was a curious incident in the course of that match. Park and I halved the first ten holes (a sequence without parallel, I think, in an event of the kind), and it was at the eleventh, where the succession of halves ended, that the strangest thing in the match happened.

Park had driven, and his ball was lying far up the fairway. I drove, and my ball pitched plump on top of his and knocked it forward. But for the fact that there were fore-caddies, we should have known nothing of the collision, for we could not see it from the tee. His ball was replaced in its original position, and in the end he secured the hole. We had a terrific struggle that day at North Berwick, and I managed to finish two up. Park was not at his best when the second half of the match took place at Ganton, and as I was in the happy mood of being unable to do the wrong thing (we all have these pleasant attacks occasionally), I won pretty comfortably.

I shall never forget the first caddie that ever I had in a championship. The occasion was the meeting at

Prestwick, Scotland, in 1893, and my henchman was a hunchback about twelve years of age. He insisted on my taking his advice in regard to every shot that I played, and, being young at the time, I obeyed him faithfully. At length, however, we came to a situation in which I did not in the least fancy his scheme for my good, and, ignoring his counsel, I executed the stroke that appealed to me. His disgust was complete. From that moment he would have scarcely anything to do with me for the remainder of the championship. To be sure, he fulfilled his contract by continuing to carry my clubs, but he would not so much as take one out of my bag. Every time we came up to the ball he turned his back on me and held the bag at arm's length for me to select whatever club I might desire. It was useless to ask him for a hint. Such sustained and dignified indignation I have seen in no other boy of twelve.

He was something like the average caddie in the United States, who, so far as my experience goes, is a monument of independence. When first the British golfer plays in the States, nothing astonishes him more than the completeness with which the American caddie has succeeded in establishing his task as an easy one. He seems to be a firm believer in the theory that it is wise for every player to tee his own ball.

So it is, but I know a good many British golfers who would rather have a tee made badly than go to the trouble of preparing a proper one for themselves. The American caddie has a soul above club-cleaning—a task which is considered part and parcel of the caddie's duties at the end of a round in Britain. In the United States, I understand, the professional is usually considered responsible for it, and employs a special staff to have it done.

To one caddie whom I had in America, I handed a ball and asked him to remove the mud which had clung to it as the result of a visit to a ditch. He took it without saying a word. A few holes later, I told him that I would use it again. He produced it, still covered with mud.

"Why, you haven't cleaned it," I protested. "Haven't had time," he replied with engaging seriousness. As he had had nothing else to do but walk, I hardly knew where to start an argument with him on the subject, so I said nothing.

The keenest caddie I ever saw in America was the diminutive "Eddie" Lowry, who carried for Francis Ouimet when the latter beat Edward Ray and me for the Open Championship of the United States at Brookline, Massachusetts, in 1913. "Eddie" was about ten years of age, and he looked less. He was hardly as big as the bag which he lugged around the course, and even in the strain of the struggle, one could not help smiling when he emerged from the great crowd, grappling earnestly with his load, and made his way up to his six-feet-high employer. If the fate of America had depended upon "Eddie" that day, he could not have been keener. Much more typical of the caddie in the States was, I think, the one who said cheerfully to me in the middle of a round at Miami: "Here, hold these clubs; I'll go and kill a snake for you."

In some respects the most trying ordeal through which I ever passed was presented in a sporting goods store in Boston, during my first tour in the States over twenty years ago. The story may not be a new one, but perhaps it will be worth telling. The golf boom in America was just beginning to be something really big, and the manager of the store conceived the idea of my playing shots into a net erected in one of the showrooms. He offered me so handsome a reward for the exhibition that no sane professional would have refused it, and on the appointed day, I duly put in an appearance, ready to begin proceedings as arranged at half-past nine in the morning. The plan was that I should hit shots into the net for half an hour, rest for half an hour, begin again, and so on till five o'clock came.

The room was packed (there must have been some hundreds of people present all the time), and at the end of the first thirty minutes, I retired in accordance with the program.

Greatly to my astonishment the spectators broke into thunderous applause; they clapped, cheered, and thumped their sticks and umbrellas on the floor with such persistency that I had to return. After another spell of about half an hour I again retired, but the appreciation was as embarrassing as in the former interval, and I was obliged to resume immediately.

People were constantly coming and going, but the fresh arrivals seemed to be as satisfied as their predecessors, and I did not obtain five minutes' rest. What anybody can have seen in the performance I do not know—driving a ball into a net is hardly thrilling—but I had to do it all day.

Seeking variety, I started to play some mashie shots at taps in the ceiling, and had just struck one of those objects when the manager rushed up to implore me to desist. It appeared that if I happened to turn on the tap connected with the fire extinguisher, it would flood the store!

At about four o'clock I felt that I had had enough of it. I made my customary exit; the applause restarted, but once I was out of the showroom, I fled from the building. Nobody could have continued the game any longer.

The manager told me afterward that during the day they sold every club in the shop. That will give you some idea of the enthusiasm with which golf was taken up in the early days of its boom in America.

Golf shots sometimes meet with strange fates, and I think that the queerest I ever played was at St. Andrews. I was doing a good round until I came to the last hole. On the right of the course at this hole is a row of houses, but they are so far away as usually to be safe. On this occasion, however, I imparted so terrific a slice to my ball that it landed on top of one of the buildings, bounced down, and finished its career in a drainpipe.

An errant shot that had a happier ending was one which I saw played at Ganton, in Yorkshire, when I was professional there. A golfer hit a tee shot which struck a caddie on the head, whence it rebounded onto the clubhouse, and from there onto the green, where it lay within easy holing distance. We all expected to see the caddie drop in a stunned condition, but he stood his ground and, on being presented with a sovereign by the relieved player, he said with a grin: "Have another try!"

They were interesting days at Ganton. We had

time for a variety of sports, and an event in which golfers played no small part was an annual Christmas Day football match between Ganton and the neighboring village of Sherburn. I captained Ganton for two years, but it was not during my period in that responsible position that a local plasterer was drafted into our side in order to fill an eleventh-hour vacancy. He was a huge fellow, and he was placed at fullback with instructions to allow no opponent to pass him. He was entirely innocent of the rules of football, but he carried out his commission with a vengeance. He never went for the ball; he simply hurled himself pell-mell at any rival who came his way, and the results were alarming. Two of our opponents had to be assisted off the field, and most of the others were more or less injured. For those of us who had the playing of golf to consider, it was fortunate that he was on our side and not against it.

A singular incident occurred once when I was playing Willie Fernie, Open Champion in his day, on the Timperley course, Manchester. Fernie hit his ball close to a spot at which a horse was feeding. The animal looked curiously at the white sphere; then the demon of mischief seemed suddenly to take possession of it. Grabbing the ball in its mouth, the horse galloped off with it at top speed a full half-mile.

If ever the spirit of practical joking was reflected on the countenance of an animal, it was depicted on that horse's face as it dashed off with the ball.

Nobody knew quite what ought to be done, and in the end Fernie dropped another ball as near as possible to the spot from which the original one was purloined, and continued the game as though nothing had happened. That would be the correct procedure under the present rules. I rather fancy it was contrary to the law of those days, but it was equitable.

From time to time one sees some extraordinary golfing styles, and a player who used to fascinate me by the weirdness of his methods was a man who could only hit the ball with the top of the clubhead—that is to say, on the part where the maker's name is inscribed on the driver. That may sound incredible, but it is true. How he did it I do not know, but the fact remains that he was incapable of striking the ball with the face of the instrument or even with the sole, which would have produced a topped shot. He hit it every time right on the top surface of the head, and the consequence was that he could not use iron clubs; there was not enough striking surface—on top!

Even when he was under a hedge, he would call for a spoon, and in some wonderful manner scoop the ball up by making the impact with the top part of the head. He wore the name off his clubs in a few weeks, for he was a regular and enthusiastic player, and he never varied in his methods.

There were times when, in playing for a green, he would strike out in such unexpected directions as to work his way all around the place at which he was aiming before he finally reached it. He would invade the fairways of four or five other holes in the vicinity, and pursue his checkered career by way of bunkers, ponds, and a dozen other places of punishment intended for errant shots, at holes some distance away. I saw him once work his way around all four sides of a green before finally he got onto it. His patience was monumental, and in some of his rounds, he must have walked quite double the normal distance. He was a real enthusiast.

Long enough have we been reminiscent. I would ask you to turn again to the serious business of this chapter—the part that has to do with how to use the mashie.

A STUDY OF PUTTING

The method that succeeds

CHAPTER VI

A STUDY OF PUTTING

The method that succeeds

I AM NOT sure that there is any golden rule for achieving success on the putting green. A few well-defined principles there are that seem to have logic on their side, but they are only part of the constitution of that dispensation which we call deadly putting. The rest of the formula is a matter of individuality which cannot be communicated to anybody; it has to be born in a person.

I am far from suggesting that it is impossible to improve one's putting. Indeed, I know no detail of the game in which practice is of greater value. But that is mainly because it enables each player to discover for himself just what special characteristics he possesses in the business of laying the ball dead from a distance of twenty yards, or holing out with certainty at a range of one yard—to learn how he is meant by nature to accomplish these tasks. Different golfers accomplish them in many different ways as regards their stances, grips, and methods of hitting the ball.

Putting is the department of golf which, more

than any other, lends itself to experimentation and the exploitation of pet theories. So far as concerns the manner in which you stand, and the style in which you hold the club, and the sort of putter that you use (so long as they are not downright ridiculous), I am convinced that fancy may be allowed a fairly free rein. The all-important matter is to light upon a method that gives you the feeling that you are going to succeed, and then to practice it.

I doubt if any two people have precisely the same touch, which is a matter of supreme moment in putting. It represents the communication of the temperament and the nervous system in their most sensitive form to the act of striking a ball. Touch is of less account where the longer shots are concerned, because of the necessity of firm hitting.

In putting, it is delicacy in striking and a happy merging of caution into boldness in the mental attitude that produces the desired effect. Some things— such as swaying the body during the movement of the club—are bad, but the question as to what is good opens up a wide field for exploration in which everybody can spend an interesting hour. What I would propose is that, when the player has discovered the method that gives him the greatest confidence, he should remain faithful to it unless it fails him long and badly at some later stage, and practice it for a quarter of an hour whenever he has the opportunity. In these periods he will learn much as to the strength that is required in striking the ball and the degree of "borrow" that is necessary on sloping greens—that is, if he pursues his studies, as he should do, on a green which boasts a certain amount of undulation.

Whenever I discuss this subject, I am reminded of an elderly amateur who used to play on the MidSurrey course, near London, and who was wont to astonish strangers by his putting procedure. One day he was engaged in a match with a member of the Royal and Ancient Club who prided himself on being steeped to the fingertips in the traditions of the game. On the first three greens the elderly gentleman, standing conspicuously straddle-legged, as was his custom, holed long putts—all with his driver. "Look here," said the St. Andrews visitor, "do you use that thing for short putts as well?"

"Short putts?" repeated the local eccentric. "Haven't I had a short putt yet? No, of course, I haven't. Oh, I always take this for short putts"—and, diving to the bottom of his bag, he produced a specimen of the ordinary household hammer!

I hesitate to think that anybody need have gone to such extremes as these, but there is every reason why the player should select the club that takes his fancy, whether it be made of wood, iron, or aluminum, without paying slavish attention to the types preferred by other and possibly better golfers.

Perhaps I need not remind the reader that my reputation as a holer-out is deplorable. How many short putts I have missed during the past fifteen or twenty years I should not like to estimate. They must number thousands. Once you lose your confidence near the hole, you are in a desperate plight, especially when you have a reputation to uphold and you know that a putt of two feet counts for as much as the most difficult iron shot. Nobody can say that a putt of this length calls for any real skill at golf; it simply demands confidence.

People who happen to have seen much of my play, tell me that in approach-putting I need not desire to be better than I am, and personally I am well satisfied with my form in this part of the game. So that perhaps I may, without presumption, offer a few hints as to how to lay the ball by the holeside from anywhere near the edge of the green. I am convinced that absolute stillness of the head and body is essential. One or two good putters there are who sway forward as they strike the ball, but they are such very rare phenomena as only to accentuate the importance to the ordinary mortal of the still head and body.

The stance may be that in which the player feels most comfortable, although I certainly do not believe in standing with the feet far apart. Rather would I go to the other extreme, and have the heels touching. This, however, is largely a matter of personal choice. If you keep the head and the body absolutely still, and take the club back so that it is not pushed outward away from the feet but inclines rather to come in slightly in the backswing, you ought to hit the ball in a straight line. And that is obviously the first essential of successful putting. Judgment of strength must come with practice.

When I was younger, I putted in a manner which was really a concentrated form of what is known as the push shot. I addressed the ball with the hands a little in front of it, so that the face of the club was tilted over in a slight degree on to the ball. As the club was a putting cleek with a trifle of loft on it, this tilting over produced the effect of a straight-faced club, and I simply came down onto the back of the ball, and away it would speed with backspin—either to the holeside or into the tin.

This principle suited me extremely well for years, but I changed it ultimately in favor of a smooth, pendulum swing; the arms moving backwards and forwards to swing the club, and the head and body being perfectly still. I think it is the soundest system; certainly it has suited me remarkably well in playing all kinds of long putts, and the reason I have missed so many short ones has been mainly a tendency to lift the head with a jerk through that "jump" which one experiences when one fears suddenly that a shot is going wrong.

I am a wholehearted believer in the overlapping grip for putting, and even the person who does not fancy it in driving can adapt himself easily to it on the green. It promotes that unison of the hands which is so important, for if you have the two hands working independently in ever so slight a degree in the delicate business of controlling a putt, the result is nearly sure to be disastrous.

Examine the line only from the ball; never from the hole. The confusion that results from studying the line from both ends is embarrassing beyond words; whenever I have done it, I have seen different lines, and that observed from the hole has proved to be the wrong one.

The bugbear of the short putt is, perhaps, that one is apt to exaggerate its difficulties. The longer one looks at it the greater appear to become little undulations in the line, until in the end one tries to do cleverly, by "borrowing," that which might be

THE PUTTER

ILLUSTRATIVE CHART

A LONG PUTT.—(1) In the stance and address the ball should be near-ly opposite the right heel, the heels being close together. This club should be used with the same movement and rhythm as the pendulum of a clock.

A LONG PUTT.—(2) The photograph shows the backswing, which involves a very slight turn of the hips. The position of the arms produce the beginning of a pendulum swing.

A LONG PUTT.—The finish. The clubhead has followed through as nearly as possible on the line of the putt and has risen slightly from the ground.

accomplished easily with a straightforward, confident shot of strength calculated to send the ball firmly to the back of the tin.

It is a nice question as to the precise stage at which a sense of dignity should restrain a golfer from gratifying little whims which, in his opinion, would help his game without contravening the rules.

Thus, I witnessed not long ago a novel method of dealing with those troublesome trifles—short putts. At least, it was novel as regards the nature of the implement with which it was performed. The shaft and the blade of the club constituted a sharp right angle. The heel was absolutely square. It was a weapon that might have been made as a cubic caricature of an ordinary putting cleek; it scorned the idea of rounding off corners.

Obviously, however, it was not illegal according to the letter of the law. Nor was the manner of using it, which was the same as that adopted several years ago by a coterie of people in Britain who employed croquet mallets as putters.

The player stands full-faced to the hole, his two feet more or less parallel to the line which he proposes to take, and swings the club between his legs. He does not swing it very far, because he employs it only, I think, for short putts. As a means of mastering those sometimes demoralizing nuisances, he claims that it is preeminent. A famous golfer said some time ago, that if he had the pluck to be seen with such a thing, he would use it every time he found himself close to the hole and under the absolute necessity of getting the ball down to avoid losing.

One advantage claimed is that in facing the hole and pushing the arms straight out instead of standing sideways and swinging the arms alongside the body, the player virtually disposes of the danger of allowing one hand to work against the other. The wrists have little chance of taking charge of the situation. The main idea is that you can only be sure of obtaining the pendulum action by standing full face to the hole and letting the arms move out and back again in front of the body. It is contended that the practice of swinging the arms from side to side is utterly unsuited to the purpose, and that people adopt it for no better reason than that it is necessary for the longer shots. Putting, it is pointed out by the daring innovator, is different from anything else in the game, and calls for an entirely different process.

This is mostly theory, but the independent soul who has had the courage to put it to the test has prospered exceedingly on his unorthodoxy, and he now walks about the links apparently immune from the terrorizing influence which a four-foot putt is apt to exercise on the average person who is under the necessity of holing it for a half.

Whether our good friend, the inventor, is really playing golf as it is supposed to be played, I will not attempt to decide. An ex-champion who coquetted with the club and the stance concluded his experiment with the remark that he wished he had the cheek to try it in a championship, but it would be hard to settle from that sentiment whether he regarded it as a mere piece of impudence or a worthy means spoilt only by its alarming unconventionality.

Certainly in the laws there is nothing to say how a person shall stand to play any shot, and it is obvious that this square-headed putter is not contrary to anything that appears under the heading of "Form and Make of Golf Clubs." Indeed, the only heresy is contained in the manner of standing, which is painfully like the freakish method of the one-time mallet adherents.

Whether, however, it is reasonable to object to the manner in which a man disposes his feet and arms, especially for the tricky business of holing short putts, is a moot point. If he believes in the pendulum swing, perhaps he ought to be allowed to work out his salvation in his own way.

The late Tom Ball, twice runner-up in the British Open Championship, was one of the finest putters in the world, and he used to express frank and whole-hearted disapproval of the pendulum swing, which, he considered, tended to make a player tighten all his muscles when putting, and so develop a condition of tautness in which he could not strike the ball smoothly and easily. Ball put his case convincingly, but I do not think his method of swaying through with the club would suit the ordinary golfer. For the great majority, the idea of the pendulum swing is absolutely sound. The arms travel to and fro like the wire on which the clockweight is suspended. The frame remains still.

That, at least, is the faith of thousands of players, and if one of them has found a way of making it work well by standing facing the hole, he is hardly to be blamed for putting his discovery into operation. After all, we do sometimes find that a clock which is recalcitrant when it is standing in its proper position will begin to tick right merrily when we turn it onto its side or make it lie down on its face. Why this is I do not know; but it is conceivable that there are human beings whose works are similarly capricious, and who cannot be sure of obtaining the proper movement of the machinery unless they humor their constitutions.

Thus, Captain H. E. Hambro, a good putter, used

to stand conspicuously straddle-legged, on the principle that it was then impossible for him to sway his body during the swing. Many players who are equally good believe that one of the secrets of success is to place the heels close together. Some golfers have faith in the square stance; others stand so very open as to be at least half facing the hole in the address. There seems to be no reason why a person should not go the whole hog, and, making a full left turn, unabashedly face the hole. I dare say that a lot remains to be learned about putting.

Personally, I have made successful experiments at times—in public matches, it may be added—with left-handed putting. I have adopted this expedient when a right arm "jump" has been causing me to clutch the club extra tightly with the right hand the instant before the impact. Nearly every golfer has experienced this "jump" at some time or other; it is born of over-anxiety to do well, and is uncontrollable.

On the first occasion that I stood the wrong way around for putting—it was an exhibition match against, I think, Braid—I holed a putt of three yards. It is a very revolutionary remedy, but as half the bad putting is brought about by gripping too tightly with one hand or the other at the critical period of the stroke, almost any means of checking it is worth trying.

The overlapping grip discourages an unduly tight hold of the club, and, for that reason, it is a very good grip for putting, even in the case of golfers who do not like it when playing long shots. Tom Ball, whom I mentioned previously as a heretic on the subject of the pendulum swing, once related to me how he became converted to the overlapping grip.

On the eve of an important event, Ball was pumping the tire of his bicycle, when he ran the pump deeply into the fleshy part of the right hand, just below the thumb. He was anxious to take part in the competition, but he soon discovered that, with the ordinary palm grip, the pressure necessary with the right hand merely to enable him to keep control of the club caused great pain.

The overlapping grip, in the exercise of which the injured portion naturally rested upon the comparatively sympathetic flesh of the left thumb, afforded him considerable relief. He decided to employ it. He never afterward abandoned it.

Ball had another story showing the efficacy of accidents as cures for golfing ills. When he was professional at the West Lancashire Club, near Liverpool, he often played with an esteemed doctor whose chief fault on the links was, in the opinion of Ball, that he jammed his right thumb too firmly on the handle of the club. He pressed so hard with it that, toward the top of the swing, the thumb and the club were apt to be fighting against one another.

The victim, however, seemed unable to rid himself of his vice. One day retribution overtook the thumb. Its owner ran a needle into it. He did not commit this act of malice aforethought on the principle that a desperate remedy might cure a desperate disease; it was an accident which caused him considerable annoyance at the time, since he had arranged to play golf on that very morning. He explained what he had done, and that he would have to give up the idea of going out for a round.

"Not at all," said Ball. "You've done the best thing in the world for yourself. You won't be able to press with the right thumb now." The lucky doctor went out and showed excellent form. And so happiness was brought to another soul.

Then there is the interesting case of Mr. Harold H. Hilton, who, at a time when the surgeon had forbidden him to play golf at all, accomplished what he has described as the best performance of his life. Most people who have studied the history of the game know that the rivalry between Mr. Hilton and the late Lieut. F. G. Tait was exceptionally keen. They met fairly often in various events, but for some strange reason, their struggles nearly always ended in the discomfiture of Mr. Hilton. Only once did he succeed during the period in which Lieut. Tait occupied a position in the front rank of golfers, and that occasion was presented at the very time when Mr. Hilton was supposed to be nursing an injured hand.

The competition was for the St. George's Cup at Sandwich. The season was 1894. Some weeks before the meeting, Mr. Hilton badly tore the main sinew leading from the thumb and forefinger to the wrist. He was ordered by the surgeon to give up golf for a long while, and not to think of carrying out his idea of competing for the St. George's Cup.

Being as keen as he was human, he ignored the advice. From the time of the accident until he reached Sandwich, he did not use his injured hand; then he used it to such good purpose that he won. He was coupled with Lieut. Tait, and with a score of 167, the Englishman gained by three strokes the one and only sweet triumph over the favorite enemy.

In all these cases the players had to adopt a light grip, for the simple reason that their injuries prevented them from holding tightly, and I venture to say that they discovered something as to its merits, especially in putting. It is an involuntary tightening of the grip during the putting swing that causes the body to become rigid, and it is when the body is rigid that it is most likely to move.

I am sure that all my bad short putts—and they have been many—have been the result of moving the body, which has been the outcome of the right arm "jump" and consequent tightening of the grip. Some very excellent putters—I would mention Willie Park and Arnaud Massy as examples—find that they obtain the best results, especially in playing long putts, by imparting a little "pull" to the ball. It is done by striking the ball nearer to the toe than the heel of the clubface; the mere act of following through in a rhythmic way secures the effect of "pull" so long as the impact occurs near the toe of the club. It is worth trying by the golfer who is inclined to "cut" his putts, for that, I think, is the worst thing possible with the modern ball, although Jack White used to practice it very effectively with the old ball. I place my faith nowadays in striking the ball with the middle of the clubface, swinging pendulum-like, and keeping the sole of the putter close to the ground throughout the swing.

Golf, for all the appearance of tame tranquillity that it is apt to present to the uninitiated mind, provides a more searching test of nerve and temperament than any other game in the world. That, indeed, is the opinion of most people who are experienced in the pursuit of sports and pastimes, and it is the cause of a phenomenon which offers much food for reflection. Golf is unique in the respect that it has two types of first-class players who are in the same grade so far as concerns the ability to hit the ball with complete skill and in perfect style, but who differ entirely in the results which they achieve in important events. One party can win championships, and the other party cannot for the life of it do anything of the kind. Yet to the person who has studied the methods of the less-fortunate individuals, there seems at first blush to be no way of accounting for their failures.

In a comparatively minor competition or a practice round, they play in a manner which suggests that they are capable of succeeding in the strongest company and on any occasion. They execute the most intricate shot with ease and grace; it is impossible to be other than enthusiastic about their gifts. Somehow, when they make their efforts in classic tournaments, they prove deficient with a regularity that is distressing. To mention names would be invidious; every devotee of the game knows that there are truly great golfers who never secure championships, and who exhibit such characteristics that, after a while, they are hardly so much as expected to win. Yet all the time they are recognized as brilliant players.

Something is lacking in their nerve or temperament (the words, I suppose, are synonymous), and it is interesting to consider the various phases of this strange condition of affairs.

Personally, I am satisfied that in order to be a champion, a person must have a good deal of sensitiveness in his nervous system. The man of sluggish disposition, the player with a truly "phlegmatic temperament" (that phrase which is so often used approvingly in regard to the individual who remains outwardly calm in a crisis), would not be likely to rise to greatness on the links. Of all games, golf is the one that comes nearest to being an art. It is pursued with deliberation and method; its inspirations are the player's own creation, since he is never called upon to strike a moving ball the action of which has been influenced by his rival. It demands the greatest delicacy and accuracy of touch, as well as, in many circumstances, the power to hit hard. An art requires a sensitive nervous system, and in golf the difference between the two sections of first-class players to whom I have referred is, presumably, that one can keep its nerves under control during the most trying period and the other cannot.

I have seen men positively trembling with excitement at the critical stage of a contest, and yet possessed of such command over themselves as to be able to play every shot perfectly. This is just about as valuable a gift as the championship aspirant can possess, and to express surprise at a person's deficiency in regard to it is just about as reasonable as to be astonished at his inability to disperse a headache by willpower. For the great majority of people, it is in connection with short putts that nerves attain their most painful activity; there is nothing else in sport quite like the short putt at golf. You know that there can be no reasonable excuse for failing to knock a ball into a hole four feet distant, and yet there is a considerable chance of failing. And the higher the reputation of the player and the more, therefore, that is expected of him, the greater are the trials of the short putt. For all the skill that it requires he has no advantage over the twenty-four-handicap man, and he realizes that, if he misses it, there will be no chance of recovery. It will be a hole lost or a stroke gone.

In all sincerity I express the opinion, after having undertaken three lengthy tours in the United States, that American golfers are better holers-out than British golfers. They are the cooler on the putting greens, and, after all, absence of anxiety is the chief essence of success.

Without doubt successful putting is mainly a matter of confidence, and that several great golfers fail to win championships by reason of their weakness near the hole is probably due to the fact that they have never gained complete confidence in their ability to get down a four-foot putt. For many happy years it did not so much as enter my head that I could miss a short putt, except as the result of carelessness; then I struck a bad patch in this hitherto simple business. The result was that there developed in my right forearm a nerve which puzzled a good many medical friends and subjected me to indescribable mental torture. Whenever I prepared to play a short putt (it was only close to the hole that I had any trouble, so that the affliction must have been born largely of imagination and environment), I would wait for that nerve in the right arm to jump. The instant I felt it was about to start, I would make a dash at the ball in a desperate effort to be in first with the shot, and what happened as a consequence of this haste may be readily imagined.

Occasionally, the "jump" would leave me entirely for a month or two. Early in the final round of the Open Championship at Prestwick, in 1914, the wretched thing suddenly reasserted itself. I felt the "jump" with a thrill of apprehension that is far from being a pleasant memory. Anyhow, the main point was not to let my partner and only formidable rival at that stage, J. H. Taylor, know anything about it. He was as well aware as I that if the distress became serious, I could miss putts down to six inches; it was strange to be walking along reflecting earnestly that not the smallest inkling of this development must be allowed to reach Taylor's ears, lest it should stimulate him to believe, as almost certainly it would have done, that he had me as good as beaten. Perhaps it was just this diversion from the thought of the possibilities of the jump itself, that enabled me partially to overcome it and to struggle home first.

As a test of nerve, that last day's play at Prestwick was far and away the most trying I can remember. That we should have drawn ahead of the other competitors and then been drawn together for the final rounds was in itself sufficient to agitate either of us to the utmost; that we should have been struggling for the honor of a sixth victory in the championship (each of us, and also James Braid, having previously won five times) filled the cup of excitement to overflowing. I know that I played one shot without seeing the ball at all. It was buried in fine, loose sand, in a bunker to the left of the eleventh green, and close to the face of the hazard. The sand was scraped away from the top of the ball, but it was so loose that it closed over the object again. I simply could not wait; I swung, guessing and hoping, and fortunately hit the shot all right.

That was an exceptional occasion. In the ordinary way, I bear constantly in mind the conviction that the best way to win any important event is to play just as one would play a private round at home, and not endeavor to accomplish the performance of a lifetime. There is such a thing as trying too hard; it begets anxiety, which is usually fatal—especially in putting.